Praise for *The Pig and the Python*

"A timely and engaging analysis of the impact of changing demographics on personal investment planning."
—David K. Foot, author of *Boom, Bust and Echo*

"An illuminating tale of a boomer couple preparing for a secure future."
—David Chilton, author of *The Wealthy Barber*

"Baby boom trends are the key to creating wealth. This fascinating book tells you how."
—Harry Dent, Jr., author of *The Great Boom Ahead and the Roaring 2000s*

"…the rarest of offerings, a financial planning primer that doesn't double as a cure for insomnia."
—*The Record*, Kitchener

D1509529

Bulls, Bears and Pigs

HOW TO FIND BALANCE IN YOUR FINANCIAL LIFE

David Cork

KEY PORTER BOOKS

Library and Archives Canada Cataloguing in Publication

Cork, David
Bulls, bear and pigs : how to find balance in your financial
life / David Cork.

Includes bibliographical references.
ISBN 1-55263-641-0

1. Financial security. 2. Investments. 3. Retirement income—Canada—Planning.
I. Title.

HG179.C659 2004   332.024'01'0971   C2004-906456-8

The publisher gratefully acknowledges the support of the Canada Council for the Arts and the Ontario Arts Council for its publishing program. We acknowledge the support of the Government of Ontario through the Ontario Media Development Corporation's Ontario Book Initiative.

We acknowledge the financial support of the Government of Canada through the Book Publishing Industry Development Program (BPIDP) for our publishing activities.

Key Porter Books Limited
Six Adelaide Street East, Tenth Floor
Toronto, Ontario
Canada M5C 1H6

www.keyporter.com

Text design: Peter Maher
Electronic formatting: Jean Lightfoot Peters

Printed and bound in Canada

05 06 07 08 09 6 5 4 3 2 1

*We've shared bull markets, bear markets
and all markets in between. You've allowed me to
share your dreams and aspirations, your joys and tragedies,
your family arrivals and departures.
You've challenged and inspired me, and I've valued your
insight and your friendship. Thank you for your continued
support and confidence in me. I have always tried to give you
my best. You are the reason that after twenty-one years,
I still love to go to work every day.
I dedicate this book to my clients.*

Contents

Introduction

"Bulls make money, bears make money, pigs get slaughtered." This phrase is used in the investment industry as a warning of the perils of acting in an overly greedy manner in the markets. In recent years, we have witnessed unprecedented volatility in the markets, characterized by spectacular highs and devastating lows. Those who get greedy lose money. But on the flip side, those who are fearful of the volatility also lose money.

Fear and greed are nothing new to the financial markets, where the optimistic bulls battle the pessimistic bears for control of public sentiment and market direction. What's new is the arrival of our third beastly metaphor, the pig. Almost a decade ago, I likened our largest generation—the baby boomers—to a pig passing through a python. The large bulge in the python's belly represents the enormous girth of the baby boom generation. The python represents the economy. One media pundit has suggested that the snake swallowed the pig to the mutual discomfort of both.

The baby boomers are well educated, they are confident, and they are more affluent at this stage of their lives than any previous generation has been. But middle age is a challenging time for a group of people who swore never to trust anyone over the age of thirty. This is a time when our baby boomers need to take stock. They have worked, on average, for twenty years and likely have at least twenty to go. They are also at the halfway point in their lives. As they watch their children struggle to become adults, the boomers also face aging parents. The demands of two generations are tugging at them. So here they sit in the locker room of life, at halftime, reflecting on what they have learned and what challenges lie ahead.

The media have wrongly characterized this generation as staring down early retirement. Boomers are not "acting their age." But we need to be mindful of what they're doing and how they're feeling. They went to school late, graduated late, went to work late, left adolescence late, married late and reproduced late. They are unlikely to retire early. While they are no longer young, they still think they are—and they are certainly not old. In fact, the average boomer is still in his or her mid-forties, and is just now beginning to think about planning for retirement, both economically and emotionally.

The serendipitous nature of life always amazes me. Not so long ago, I was playing golf with a friend and his colleague. Because of my vocation, a heated debate developed over the reliability and stability of the capital markets. It was then that I asked the fateful question: "What are you doing in the market?" To my surprise, my playing partner started to rattle off his positions and the catastrophes he had endured. I asked my question again, pointing out that what I had intended to ask was his purpose in being there. Again to my surprise, he was stymied.

Subsequently, I repeated this question to a number of people I knew with the same result. This observation led to the main thesis of this book. We lack process in our approach to the capital markets and, given their difficult nature, this sets us up for less-than-desirable results. I would also contend that self-directed investing without a specific action plan is at best a recipe for underperformance and at worst a setup for potential disaster. I believe one of the reasons that boomers have had mixed results in the markets is that self-directed investing is contrary to the impulses of human nature.

In *Bulls, Bears and Pigs*, I have two main objectives. The first is to discuss the issues and struggles we all face as we try to accumulate the wealth we need to finance our lives. The second is to offer up a specific course of action that will lead us to better control over our financial decisions and, ultimately, to the success we are seeking. We can start by addressing these questions:

- What have we learned from the boomers in their initial years in the markets?
- What does smart money management look like?
- How can Canadians build and sustain wealth as they approach retirement?
- Will aging change the way we invest?

Readers of my first two books, *The Pig and the Python* and *When the Pig Goes to Market*, will recognize many of the characters in this book. Making a return appearance are:

HAZEN ARMSTRONG: Our demographer, who studies the boomers and offers his theories on their impact.

Ruth Schneider: Hazen's wife, recently retired from the University of Ottawa. A sociologist by training, she is very interested in the social aspects of the lives of our largest generation.

Pieter and Meredith DeMarco: Our mainstream boomers. Their lives are characterized by the social and financial vagaries of being part of our largest generation.

Dylan Armstrong: Ruth and Hazen's son and a member of Generation X. Dylan offers his insights into the baby boomers from the perspective of the generation below them.

In addition, *Bulls, Bears and Pigs* introduces a couple of new faces:

Andrew Proctor: A baby boomer himself, Andrew is an investment broker who acts as a financial advisor for Hazen and the DeMarcos.

Jamie Arsenault: A financial planner who attempts to put Pieter and Meredith on the right path to proper money management.

Canada is changing. Our population is aging, and our cultural mosaic continues to evolve as new Canadians arrive on our shores. We will face challenges both as a country and as individuals. The key to success is to pay attention to the trends going on around us, stay flexible and have a plan. It is my strong belief that age will not be wasted on the elderly. Wisdom and experience will pay off in spades.

1
Miles to Go

HAZEN

Winter sometimes seems to drag on forever. But inevitably there's that one day when the weather starts to shift. The sun is out, the birds are back, there's a fresh smell in the air, and you know winter is on the run at last. When the first true spring day arrives, you wake up with an all-consuming thought: it's time to go play golf.

I didn't really understand golf when I was younger. I had played off and on, but I never really got the bug. Then, about ten years ago, a friend of mine who belonged to one of the old established clubs asked if I might consider joining. I had never thought about joining a club, but the offer was interesting. The clubhouse was a classic, the course was spectacular, and I knew many of the members.

Of particular interest to me, given my line of work, was that most of the new members were baby boomers. For more than thirty years I've been studying the effects of the boomers on the economy. The boomers, those born between 1947 and 1965, are such a large cohort—nine million strong, more than 30 percent of the Canadian population and larger than either the generation before it or the one following it—that the choices they make as they progress through life have a huge impact on the investment markets. This first occurred to me back in the mid-sixties, when I learned that sales of Gerber baby food had doubled between 1948 and 1950. Since then, the boomers have influenced sales of everything from Beatles records to real estate and minivans to gardening tools. Keeping an eye on these trends—and predicting what the boomers will be drawn to next—has helped me determine where and how to invest money, and I have been able to make a career out of guiding others to informed investment decisions.

I like to think of the boomer generation as a pig being digested by the python of the Canadian economy. Right now, the pig is right in the middle of the snake's belly: a huge bulge that flattens out on either side. To me this image aptly depicts the distribution of the Canadian population, and I often use it in my lectures.

Golf is fast becoming the leisure sport of choice for our largest generation as they enter their peak earning years and start thinking about retirement, or whatever might come next in their lives. With their children gaining independence and starting to move out on their own, boomers have more time and money to spend on leisure activities. In addition, boomers are becoming concerned about staying in shape, but are a little lazy about it, preferring activities that are "actively relaxing." Golf, as a way to both relax and get some exercise, is the perfect outlet. And the golf club is the perfect place for me to observe the boomers around me.

So here I was, getting ready to head out for the first round of the year. And what a way to kick it off. I was looking forward to spending time with my son, Dylan, who had recently returned to town to start his new job. He had been travelling for a year after grad school and had landed a way-cool, as he described it, systems analyst position with Hewlett-Packard. Way-cool or not, I was just happy he was employed. And it was nice to have him in town to join me for a game of golf.

Dylan had invited his lifelong friend and partner-in-crime, Jamie Arsenault, to play with us today. Jamie had landed a great job out of college with a major investment firm. It's hard to believe that was more than seven years ago. I have enjoyed watching Dylan and Jamie together ever since they were small. They play off each other in a way that, when they were in school, sometimes resulted in chats with teachers and principals. But I always knew that their mischief was relatively harmless, and that their ability to work as a team would serve them well as they grew up.

The final member of our foursome was my friend Pieter DeMarco. We like to joke about the fact that we both have unusual names. Pieter's name is the result of being the son of a Dutch mother and an Italian father. My name, on the other hand, is simply uncommon, although a couple of prominent Canadians have shared it, such as Hazen Argue, Canada's longest-serving parliamentarian. Pieter, as an engineer, has a natural curiosity about things that I am always amused by. My wife, Ruth, and I spend a great deal of time with Pieter and his wife, Meredith, our consummate boomer friends. We met the DeMarcos about ten years ago when they moved across the street from us and Meredith and I promptly struck up a conversation. Since then, Meredith has worked with both Ruth and me, helping us with research on our various projects. A few years ago, she and Pieter bought a house a little farther away, but the friendship has remained intact, despite the twenty-year difference in our ages. Ruth has recently retired from teaching sociology at the University of Ottawa, and she shares my interest in the boomer generation. Our friendship with the DeMarcos gives us terrific insight into how the boomers face middle age.

I arrived at 7:30 to pick Pieter up for our 8:15 tee-off. As I pulled up in front of his house, he was standing at the door, chatting with Meredith. He saw my car, grabbed his golf bag and headed down the lawn. Meredith broke out in a wide grin.

"Is there something funny I should know about?" I yelled, getting out of the car.

"Oh, it's just that Pieter's a little grumpy this morning, and golf doesn't often cheer him up," she replied.

"How can you be grumpy before the first game of the year?" I asked, as Pieter dropped his clubs in the trunk.

"It's not the golf. There's just a lot going on right now, and Meredith knows that golf is not relaxing for me."

"Mindset—it controls everything we do," I replied. "How does that phrase go? 'A bad day on the golf course is better than a great day at the office.'"

I could see that jocularity wasn't going to have much of an impact on Pieter's mood, so we spent the fifteen-minute drive to the club chatting about his family. Meredith and Pieter have two children: Malcolm, who is working on a degree in history at Queen's, and Emily, who just started high school.

Pieter looked a little melancholy when I asked how the kids were doing. "You know, it's funny. Before your children head off to university, you underestimate everything: the cost, the effect it will have on your life and, mostly, how much you'll miss them. When they're born, your friends joke that they'll come home from the hospital and stay in your home forever. In reality, they stay for such a brief time."

"Your generation has fewer children than past generations did," I responded. "So you tend to focus on each child much more, and every stage in their lives and yours becomes magnified in its importance."

"I know. High-school graduation, university graduation, their first jobs—they're all huge events, as Meredith and I are discovering," Pieter replied.

"And how's Emily?"

"She's doing well. She seems to be liking school well enough, though it's hard to get kids her age to open up."

"Has she started to think about universities?"

"I think she's going to stay close to home, but we still have a couple of years to decide."

As we pulled up to the club, I could see Frick and Frack hitting balls into a net beside the putting green. It was fun to see Dylan and Jamie together again; they'd been such a team over the years. Jamie has always excelled in athletics, and it was great for Dylan to be around him. Being the only child of two older, somewhat cerebral parents can have its pitfalls, and Ruth and I had gone to great lengths to make growing up as normal as possible for Dylan. He was in Cubs, and he played on every soccer, baseball and hockey team we could find, though he's not a natural athlete. One of my friends, whose children are older, passed along one simple rule for successful child rearing: if you want to keep them out of trouble, exhaust them. They can't get into too much mischief when they're asleep. We did encourage

Dylan's friendship with Jamie despite, or perhaps because of, the trouble those two always seemed to find as kids.

"Good morning, gentlemen—and I use the term somewhat loosely. Nice to see that the two of you remembered we were playing this morning."

Dylan smiled. "He has trouble recognizing that we're now adults and can act responsibly."

Jamie nodded his head. "I know. I'm gainfully employed, I'm married, I've now reproduced. Here I am in my thirties, and my folks still think of me as a kid. I think it's a coping mechanism for them."

"It's not your age, guys," I retorted. "You may recall that I have some experience with your antics. Anyway, time's a-wasting. We've got a date on the first tee."

We walked down to the tee. As usual, it was all but abandoned. The boomers were slowly making an impact, but the club membership was still a little on the aged side. Seniors like to get up early, but not this early. It takes a while to loosen up the old bones in the morning. No problem at all for a youngster like me. One of my long-term goals is to reach the ultimate summit of the golfing world: I want to shoot my age. Now, this is tricky. I am currently sixty-eight, so I'm closing in on the front edge of this zone. To achieve this feat, you not only need to continue to be fit, but you also have to be able to play quite well. But I'm also a realist; judging by my level of play, my guess is I've got a shot if I can live to a hundred. Goals don't always have to be attainable to be useful. Every time I golf from now on, I'm out here to try to shoot my age.

We hit our balls, and it was game on.

The first few holes were rather uneventful. We indulged

in the usual golf banter: "Nice putt, Alice, did you borrow your mother's clubs? I'm not sure that's past the women's tee." It's amazing how golf, such a gentle, gentleman's game, inspires such infantile chatter. It's kind of refreshing, actually. You can revert to your childhood very quickly on the golf course. This is particularly true when a group of males is involved.

On the fairway of the fourth hole, our day took a very interesting turn. Pieter hit a shot, then turned to Jamie. "Hazen tells me you're an investment advisor with one of the major firms." Pieter had a serious look on his face as he spoke. "I'm pretty close to swearing off the stock market; in the end I think it's a bit of a crap shoot."

Jamie looked as if he'd heard this once or twice. "I can never figure out why people feel that way about the market."

"Oh, there's an easy answer: it never lives up to its billing. Rates of return never seem to come close to what was advertised," Pieter replied.

The reason Pieter was a little cranky this morning was becoming apparent. I knew he was deeply involved in the tech market, and the whole sector had been choppy of late. Jamie was experienced and could handle himself, but I was determined not to let things get out of hand.

Jamie responded, "I guess what we need to do is define what we mean by rates of return. The fact is, over the long haul, the stock market has averaged an excellent rate of return."

I could see that Pieter was starting to get engaged in this conversation. There was only one problem: it was Jamie's shot. "Okay, guys, it's wonderful to have these spirited debates, but you've got to keep hitting the ball. If the pace of play seems slow, it must be your shot."

With that, Jamie hit a beautiful high wedge onto the green, and Pieter slapped one into the bushes. Getting him out of his funk wasn't going to be easy. We finished up our hole and walked to the next tee.

Jamie looked a little sheepish. "Sorry, Pieter. I don't want to sound condescending, but I get a little pumped up when I talk about the market because it's such an interesting beast."

"I'm not sure I share your excitement," Pieter responded.

"Come on, Pieter, you're an engineer—you should find some interest in the mathematical side of the market." Jamie was pointing at Pieter's baby finger. Pieter smiled as he held up his hand. Jamie had observed the steel ring on Pieter's finger, the true sign of an engineer. "Hazen mentioned you were in tech. In the investment business, we get into the habit of checking for a ring. We have a joke that engineers are required to wear their rings when entering investment offices as a warning to us. Your ilk have a habit of being very specific and asking extraordinarily technical questions."

Pieter smiled at Jamie's joke, but seemed a bit distracted. Clearly, his mind was elsewhere.

We played the next couple of holes with relative speed and little mishap. When we approached a short par three, we caught up to the group in front of us. It seemed no one in that foursome had hit the green; in fact, none of them seemed able to locate their balls. We had a few minutes to wait, and I could see Jamie wanted to get back to the conversation. "The problem with engineers—and other investors, as well—is that they tend to overanalyze. Let me ask you a simple question, Pieter, to demonstrate my point. What are you doing in the market?"

Pieter took a moment before responding. "Well, most of my holdings are in technology, because it's an area I understand. I also have some bank stocks and some blue-chip stocks and a handful of mutual funds my advisor recommended. And I have an oil company, I think, and a gold play a friend recommended that's supposed to go big in the next year."

Jamie smiled. "No, no, you missed my point. I don't want to know what you *have* in the market. I want to know what you're *doing* in the market."

Pieter looked puzzled, as if he was struggling to understand the question.

Jamie continued, "What are you doing, what are you trying to accomplish, what's your plan, what are your goals, what does the end look like?"

"I'm trying to maximize my return."

At this point I had to cut them off. "Okay, men, simple mantra: walk-talk-shoot, walk-talk-shoot. They do like to get you off the course in four hours. If you dawdle, I get a letter from the club, and I hear those letters are very challenging to your emotional well-being."

"What are these letters all about?" Pieter asked.

"Just a leftover from the past," I replied. "I think there are 4,372 ways to be cited for improper conduct. Slow play is just one of them. If I'm wrong on that number, it's not by much."

I hated to rein them in. I liked where the conversation was headed, but we really did have to keep moving.

We paused for a drink at the end of nine holes, which gave Pieter and Jamie a chance to re-engage. "Okay, Pieter, so your main goal is to maximize your return, is that right?"

Pieter nodded.

Jamie said, "You see, that's a little like saying, 'My goal in golf is to lower my score.' So what? It's just a statement; it's not a solution. Wouldn't the solution be to play better? The key question to ask is, How? In both endeavours, playing golf and maximizing returns, hoping things will get better on their own won't work and, unfortunately, just trying harder won't work. Golf is a technical game, similar in many ways to the markets. My senior partner, Andrew Proctor, has a little chat he gives that lists the similarities between golf and investing."

"I'd love to hear that list sometime," I broke in.

"Andrew's a member here, Hazen. He's getting back into playing a bit more, now that his kids are getting older. I'm sure I can set you two up for a round."

"I'd enjoy that. I'm always interested in a game, especially when the conversation is interesting, because I certainly don't get much pleasure from my golf skill."

Jamie returned to the topic at hand, "Both golf and investing are counterintuitive, and as a result very frustrating."

"How so?" Peter asked.

"Think about it. Buy when you don't like something, sell it when you love it—tough to do. Hit down to get the ball up, swing easy to get it to go farther, relax after you've hit a bad shot—tough to do."

"I think I see what you mean." Pieter said.

"We have to learn to do the right things, and we have to do them a lot," Jamie continued. "It comes down to process.

There is no point in going to a range and hitting hundreds of balls just to reinforce a bad swing. Likewise, many investors repeat past mistakes over and over and never seem to learn. It's the old simple-versus-easy problem. The solutions for most investors are simple; in fact, they are right in front of their eyes."

I tried playing devil's advocate. "If they're so simple, Jamie, why doesn't everyone use them?"

"That's right," Pieter nodded. "Why don't investors do as well as they should?"

"As I said, the solutions are simple, but they're not easy. The day-to-day noise of the market gets in the way. Human emotions get in the way. Lack of a plan is a problem. I could go on for days. It really is about process. A golf pro would be hard pressed to help you just by describing a better swing. I'd be hard pressed to fix your investment process on the golf course. Why don't we meet in my office sometime soon and have a chat? Andrew always loves it when an engineer drops by."

"Sounds good," Pieter said.

Dylan, who had been uncharacteristically quiet for most of the round, finally had something to say. "What Jamie is saying is a lot like a number of case studies we reviewed in business school. Companies, the smart ones, are constantly looking at their processes. Not just on the production and development side, but also on delivery. How does the end user view the product?"

Jamie nodded. "That's a huge issue in our industry right now. It's unfortunate that we tend to review how we do things *after* a major event. The recent corrections in the markets have given investors occasion to review their process."

"That's how human nature works," I responded.

"It's interesting you should mention human nature, Hazen. You like to look at the baby boomers and how they influence things. They've obviously had a huge impact on the financial sector. I just read a study on how the baby boomers' first twenty years in the markets coincided with an explosion in self-directed investing. The study suggested that while the intent was to empower investors, the outcome has been less than optimal. In a nutshell, the authors suggested that human nature gets in the way of self-directed investing. The problem, it turns out, is too much choice. There are thousands of different investment options, and when we self-direct, we can choose any of them. When you throw in the volatility that 86 million boomers in North America bring to the markets, we have created a recipe for turmoil. Andrew has spent a great deal of time on this issue. I really should put you in touch with him."

"So you and Andrew feel boomers aren't measuring up in the markets?" I inquired.

"No, they're doing okay, but as they hit middle age they're going to have to do better. And keep in mind I mean they need to develop a better process and a better understanding of what they're doing and why. They need to get serious. The boomers are older and more focused, and they should be. For many, their financial well-being will depend on their ability to grasp what's going on and react appropriately.

"Point taken," Pieter said.

Jamie smiled. "That's what I love about engineers. In the end, you can always appeal to their sense of logic. If we give them the right process, they thrive."

"So we can follow up on this at your office?" Pieter asked.

"Of course. That's what I do."

As the game wound down, I kept thinking about Jamie's back-to-basics approach. It made so much sense to me, and I was surprised at myself for not clueing in to it before now. I guess I had been spending so much time on the impact the boomers would have on the markets that I had missed parts of the larger trend. I had assumed they would flood the capital markets as they had done with schools and homes and, frankly, everything else. But for many, an understanding of this commodity does not come as naturally as an understanding of real estate. A much greater effort is going to be needed by the investment industry to manage and instruct our largest generation on the appropriate approach to the markets.

I was reminded of the importance of an open mind. It's all well and good to make predictions based on demographics and history, but we can only predict so much about human behaviour. In the end, the boomers will make some unexpected choices, both in investing and in life, that will lead to unexpected outcomes.

Jamie handily won the golf game, with a final score of 78. The rest of us had struggled, as most hackers do. But we had a glorious walk in the sun.

2
Halftime

RUTH

It's amazing how time flies. Hazen and I have now been married for five full years. It took us a little longer than many couples to get to the altar; our son, Dylan, was twenty-eight before we finally took the plunge. Although we had always maintained a strong friendship and professional relationship, and had shared the responsibilities and joy of raising Dylan, we had always maintained separate residences. The sixties had a profound effect on us, I guess, and we both cherished our freedom and independence. It's probably just as well that we had our own homes when we were younger: we might have killed each other. But we have mellowed, and spending our senior years together feels comfortable to both of us.

The years seem to pass ever more swiftly as I get older, though. In the back of my mind, there is always that nagging concern: "So many things to do, so little time." So this year I kept a promise to myself and retired from the University of Ottawa after thirty years. My goodness, thirty years! On the one hand, it seems like just yesterday that I received tenure. On the other hand, when I think of the number of students I had, the papers and studies I read and the reports I wrote, it's hard to believe I packed so much into those years. I loved my years at the university, but it was time for a change.

I had a great time at the retirement parties my co-workers, students and friends threw for me. I didn't have the heart to tell my well-wishers I had no intention of sitting back and relaxing for the next twenty years or so. This was simply an opportunity to collect my pension and throw my life open to doing the work and research I wanted to do, on my own terms.

Being a sociologist, I find the concept of retirement intriguing. The idea of Freedom 55, of a long retirement filled with years of travel, golfing, gardening, bridge clubs and socializing, has now become so ingrained in our society, it's sometimes hard to remember that retirement is a relatively new phenomenon. Only in the last hundred years or so, as life expectancies rose and pensions and government programs for retirement were instituted, has retirement come to mean anything more than a few years of dependence on one's children at the end of life. According to the U.S. Bureau of Labor Statistics, in 1880, 78 percent of men were still working past age sixty-five; by 1990, that number had dropped to 20 percent. The numbers are very similar in Canada.

One contributor to the early retirement trend in the latter half of the twentieth century was the baby boom. Older workers were encouraged to move out of the workforce to make way for the enormous group moving in. They were aided in their earlier retirement by generous postwar pensions and a fortuitous windfall in real estate.

But in the last decade, another trend has started: people are continuing to work beyond the traditional age of retirement. Life expectancies in North America are still increasing, and many people are healthy and energetic well past the age of sixty-five. Knowing that their retirement could stretch out over a period of twenty years—or more— they are worried about boredom setting in if they retire too early, and they want to stay active and keep being challenged intellectually. And because many of them have struggled to save enough to last through their retirement years, they also want to keep some money coming in. A recent Statistics Canada survey confirms this trend, reporting that fully 60 percent of recent retirees wish to re-enter the workforce. In the U.S., according to a report published in 2004 by the American Association of Retired People, 80 percent of workers intend to work past the age of sixty-five or never retire.

Many workers are still leaving their full-time office jobs and collecting their pensions, but they are moving on to work part-time, either at the same type of work or at something completely different. Interestingly enough, I have noticed recently that a lot of retired people are working in retail. I guess it keeps them feeling useful, without the pressures that may have accompanied their previous jobs.

An article in the local paper suggested that the recent downturn in the investment markets was good for us. The author's reasoning was that it would force some of us to keep working. He pointed out that a reasonable amount of work is good for you: it gives you a purpose and a reason to stay connected with others.

Hopping onto the coattails of this trend, I intended to keep working for at least the foreseeable future. But not today. Spring was here, and I wanted to spend most of the day in the garden, which was slowly experiencing a makeover. You see, Hazen likes layers and complicated designs. Before I moved in, there were hardly any flowering plants in his garden, just different shades of green. I have to admit that his plants were laid out in interesting patterns, but I crave colour and fragrance! And there was no reason we couldn't add some to the mix.

Accustomed to having no one to please but himself, it took Hazen a while to accept my ideas, but he was coming around. Our one simple rule was, no tearing out until we had a consensus. It was great fun to have a good bottle of wine and a nice dinner on the patio while discussing our ideas. The only trouble was, we sometimes got so caught up in our plans, hopping up to point out this empty corner or that mass of weeds, that our food got cold.

Today, with some rare time alone in the garden, I was tidying things up, weeding and deadheading, all the while formulating plans to make the garden appealing to all the senses. I wanted more fragrant plants, and I had found a spot that would be perfect for a little herb garden, or maybe a strawberry patch—we could nibble on strawberries while we worked! And I had another idea...but I'd have to see how Hazen would react.

My garden sanctuary was breached shortly after lunch. Hazen had gone golfing that morning with our son, Dylan, and his friend Jamie. Pieter DeMarco, our former neighbour and old friend, had joined them at the last minute. I must admit, I don't understand golf. What's the line: "A good walk spoiled"? But Hazen enjoyed it, and anything that got him out of the house for a while was okay with me.

Hazen wandered into the garden, making sure no unauthorized operations had taken place in his absence.

"Good day on the course?" I asked.

"A terrific day," he replied.

"How was the group to play with?" I tried to show the appropriate spousal interest.

"Just great, actually. The golf was okay, but the discussion was a great surprise."

"And our son? How did he play?" Hazen sometimes leaves out the important details.

"Oh, Dylan played just fine. He actually had very little to say and, for a change, neither did I."

"That *is* unusual." I smiled.

Hazen smiled too. "Very unusual, but the discussion between Jamie and Pieter was fascinating."

"How so?" As usual, Hazen's unique brand of enthusiasm piqued my interest.

"Well, first, let me say Jamie has grown up to be an impressive young man. His instincts and insights were extremely interesting."

"He's working for one of the big investment firms, isn't he?" I asked, a little unsure of the details.

"Yes, that's right. He's working with one of the firm's senior partners, and it's evident he's thriving. It's nice to see someone young who has found his place and is off and running in the working world."

"Okay, so what did he say that's got you so excited?"

Hazen paused, gathering his thoughts as he often does. "Well, in a matter of a few holes, he changed the way I think about how the boomers should approach the market."

"Oh, is that all?" I laughed. I knew some of Hazen's ideas were strongly ingrained. The notion that a major plank of his work had been shifted by a morning with a member of the younger set was significant, almost amusing. Now he really had my interest. "How did he manage that?"

"It turns out Pieter has been struggling in the investment markets. Knowing that Jamie worked in an investment firm, Pieter turned his frustration with the markets on Jamie."

"And how did Jamie deal with that?"

"He did the most profound thing. He asked Pieter what he was doing in the market. And Pieter started to rhyme off all of his investments and the huge mistakes he's made and how he felt the investment advice he had received had let him down."

It didn't sound like a very pleasant chat. "Wasn't Jamie a little taken aback?"

"Not at all. In fact, it was his response that struck me. After he let Pieter blow off some steam, Jamie explained that he was not asking what securities Pieter was buying or selling, or in which sector. He wanted to know *why* Pieter was in the market, what his goals and objectives were." Hazen was becoming quite animated. "When Jamie was finished, Pieter looked bewildered. He couldn't come up with an answer right away. After a while, he suggested that his objective was to make a decent return, and Jamie jumped all over that answer. He pointed out that Pieter has no way of meeting his objective with his current course of action. The reality is, Pieter has no clear objective, and his plan of attack is ad hoc at best."

"And that was it?" I suddenly felt a little underwhelmed, like when a joke doesn't come off as funny as advertised.

"Don't you see? I always thought that when the boomers came to the market the surge in interest would drive up the values, like a rising tide lifting all the ships. We didn't focus nearly enough on the process. How could we miss it? We should have known. Boomers have always liked to do their own thing. They weren't going to quickly conform to the investing patterns of the past. They were going to reshape the market and go at it on their terms. And, as Jamie pointed out, we empowered them by throwing the investment markets open and letting them self-direct. Unfettered access, often with very little process. Pieter is a perfect example of the outcome."

Hazen sat down and sipped his lemonade for a few minutes. "So, did you tear anything out while I was gone?" he asked, with a bemused grin on his face.

"No, I know the rules. I do have some ideas, though. We still need more colour back here, and I'd like to have plants that flower at different times during the summer. I'm thinking of putting in some peonies and lilies. And there is one last touch I'd like to add."

"And what would that be?"

"A fountain," I replied. "I've been looking around at a few gardening stores for ideas. I think a multi-level number would be great for the middle of the lawn."

"And why do you want a fountain?"

"Ambience," I said. "We need a bit of gurgle back here. It's primordial. I'm a sociologist; I know these things. The sound of running water is very relaxing."

Hazen knew when he was licked. We planned an outing that afternoon to a local garden centre.

Our treasure hunt didn't take long at all. We found and agreed on a double-decker Grecian nymph arrangement fairly quickly. While we were there, I told him my idea about putting in an herb garden. It wasn't a hard sell: Hazen loves good food, and herbs fresh from the garden enhance any meal.

What Hazen had told me about his morning on the golf course kept running through my mind while we were plant shopping. It dovetailed with much of what I had been reading and thinking about lately.

We were back home by about four and got right down to business, planting our new herb garden. Hazen was gamely assisting me, but no doubt he just wanted to keep an eye on me.

"You know, there's something about what you told me that just won't let me go," I said.

"And what's that?" Hazen asked.

"I recently had a similar epiphany to the one you had this morning, only it was inspired by a couple of books. Over the last few months, as retirement approached, I found myself starting to think about what I want to do next with my life. Then a friend at the university gave me a wonderful book called *What Are You Doing after Work?* by Dr. Alan Roadburg. It was just what I needed. One sociologist advising another. He has another book out that I'd like to get my hands on—it's called *Re-tire with a Dash: The Secret to Retirement Happiness.*"

"Sounds like a book I should read too," Hazen said.

"It couldn't hurt." Hazen was only moderately amused. In many ways he views himself as part of the baby boom even though he was born a decade too soon. I went on, "The second book that inspired me was *The Progress Paradox*, by an American author, Gregg Easterbrook. The basic premise is that, by every measure, our lives have improved, and yet we are no more happy or fulfilled. In fact, we are arguably less fulfilled. We have attained the 'American dream,' and somehow it doesn't seem to have brought us any satisfaction."

"We get to the top of the mountain, look out over the world, and suddenly think, so what?" Hazen responded.

"Exactly. It sounds a lot like what you touched on during your golf game this morning. I want to study that growing phenomenon. It's almost as if the boomers lack process in life, just as they do in the investment markets. Or maybe life just got too busy or stressful."

"There's something else that strikes me," Hazen said. "I've been thinking a lot recently about faith. I know you deal with society's changing views of spiritual faith, but as boomers age, they are starting to question their faith in other institutions as well."

"You mean faith in government, faith in national organizations—"

"Faith in markets, faith in companies," Hazen cut in. "One of the great similarities between the investment market and religion is the need for faith in the unknown. In both cases, there are people who can guide us, and yet we often don't heed them."

"Interesting. Another aspect to ponder."

The afternoon folded into a perfect spring evening. The lilacs were out, and their fragrance was intoxicating. There's one great thing about being retired: no deadlines. Having worked up a great appetite, Hazen and I put some of our new herbs to good use in a marinara sauce and added whole basil leaves to our salad.

As we prepared our meal, Hazen said, "Since we're on

the topic, there's a larger issue I've been considering that ties into what Jamie had to say this morning."

"Is this going to hold up dinner?" I asked.

"No, I'll be brief," Hazen responded. "We have competing advice from Canada's two sages on the topic of demographics. In one corner we have David Foot of *Boom, Bust and Echo* fame, who suggests that demographics explain two-thirds of everything."

"And in the other corner is Michael Adams, the author of *Sex in the Snow*, who states that demographics are not destiny. Sure, you and I have talked about this many times," I said.

"Well, I've come to the conclusion that they may both be right. Because of the precise data we receive from Statistics Canada and the Census Bureau in the U.S., we know the age distribution of our population. People's ages tell us what major life moves they are likely about to make. It turns out, though, that how they go about making those moves is less clear. Think about it. We could predict that boomers would come to the real estate markets, but we couldn't predict what they'd do then, as we could with their parents. We can predict that they'll come to the financial markets, but, as Jamie pointed out, once they're in the markets they may become a little unruly. I'd like to flesh that idea out a bit more."

Dinner was ready. We set up a table in the garden, added a lovely bottle of Bordeaux, and basked in the fullness of our day and our lives.

"It's been an interesting day. You never know when ideas will pop out of the air. If you're lucky, you get to chase them and see where they go," I said.

"Uh-oh—I can tell this is leading somewhere. What's on your mind?" Hazen is always able to read me. It still surprises me how well he knows me.

"I think the time is right to pursue an idea that Meredith raised one night at dinner a few years back," I responded.

Hazen looked puzzled. "It must be the wine, but I don't remember which dinner you're referring to."

"Sure you do. She suggested that we write a book together."

"Oh, the book." Hazen smiled. "I thought it was something bigger than that."

"That *is* pretty big. I think we could write the ultimate boomer book. Here they are, at halftime in their lives, and it's okay, but they have concerns about money, lifestyle and so on." Now I was getting excited.

"*The Boomers at Halftime,*" Hazen mused. "That's a catchy title."

"I've been giving it a lot of thought lately. And the book wouldn't be just for the boomers. There are other cohorts that could use a little timely advice. One of the greatest challenges for these generations is that the world we live in is changing rapidly. Events such as 9/11 just seem to be bigger, as if the media have turned up our personal volume knob. And in many ways, we have no real role models to lean on; it's tougher to find a hero these days. Why don't we try to tackle these issues head on? We could be the Masters and Johnson of social and financial issues."

Hazen smiled. "I'll check my Daytimer to see what I'm doing for the next six months."

Retirement was definitely going to be interesting.

3
Take a Good, Hard Look

MEREDITH

My life has been quite frenzied over the past few months. Whoever said you can have it all must have had a personal valet. My master's thesis was a sprint to the finish line— probably a better idea when you're twenty-three, single and able to focus on nothing else. A little more challenging when you have a teenage daughter, a son in university, a husband trying to conquer the tech world and a forty-five-year-old body to drag around. But it was done. "Policy Choices for an Aging Population" was in the archives, ready for future generations to reflect on the utter genius of my observations.

Actually, going back to school and writing my thesis has been the fulfilment of a dream. I owe so much to Ruth and Hazen for sending me off in that direction. Life truly is serendipitous. I always thought my interest was in early childhood education, but after doing research for them my focus changed to my own cohort, the baby boomers. The proverbial oil tanker of a generation. The same kids who weren't going to trust anyone over thirty are now middle-aged and are thinking about aging, health care and retirement. But the boomers don't take the traditional approach to any stage of life. And for them, aging doesn't mean loss of function or loss of worth to society. Society is going to have to prepare itself for a new understanding of what it means to be a senior in Canada.

Now that my thesis was complete, I could actually relax for a change. Tonight was a chance for Pieter and me to catch up with Ruth and Hazen. They were due over at 7:30 to kick off the summer barbecue season. Emily was out for a movie and was staying at a friend's for the night. Malcolm had landed the ultimate summer job, driving a tour bus in Alberta. Lord knows why they trust these vehicles to young males; it gives a whole new meaning to the motto "safe, reliable and courteous." He was, however, employed for the summer, and who am I to quibble over the public's safety?

As is their habit, Ruth and Hazen arrived promptly, and as is my habit, dinner was simple: lamb, mixed veggies and one of my recent discoveries, corn on the barbecue. That way there was more time for the important stuff—chatting.

"So, how is our most recent graduate doing?" Ruth asked as she came through the door.

"Well, tired, relieved and thrilled, probably in that exact order," I responded.

"I haven't had a chance to congratulate you." Hazen leaned over to kiss my cheek.

We moved through the kitchen and out onto the back deck. I noticed that Hazen had brought a bottle of Alsace, and I ducked back into the house.

"Hazen, you'll be so proud of me," I said, walking out on the deck with my new Alsatian glasses. "These things used to be impossible to find, and suddenly they're everywhere."

"Nothing like a great wine in the perfect glass," Hazen responded.

"Tell us about your thesis," Ruth interjected. "Hazen and I have been dying to hear about it."

"I wanted to call you a hundred times to talk over my ideas, but I didn't want to bug you, given your pending retirement. I figured you'd be flooded with things that needed to be cleared up." I felt a little sheepish that I hadn't shared any of my work with Ruth.

"You're right about the flood," Ruth responded, "but you could have called any time if you needed to. And, to be clear, I'm not retiring."

I nodded. "I knew that. The real reason—and I knew you would understand—is that I needed to do this on my own. I've gained so much insight working with you and Hazen, but it was time for me to show what I can do."

"What was the title of your paper?" Hazen asked.

"Well, it's brilliant, of course," I said. "'Policy Choices for an Aging Population.'"

"Is it intended for government or business use, or does it have advice the average person would be interested in?" Ruth asked.

"Let's be honest, Dr. Schneider: other than my professor, no one is going to read this tome," I responded.

"I'm not so sure." Ruth smiled. "What were your major themes?"

"I had three. Some enormous trends are at work in Canada, and we need to acknowledge their implications. The first is that, as a society, we are slowly aging. We are living longer, and our birth rate has declined rather significantly. In fact, seniors are the fastest-growing population group. According to Health Canada, the growth of the senior population will account for nearly half of the growth of the overall Canadian population in the next four decades."

"I read some astonishing statistics on this topic lately," Ruth put in. "In 1921, one Canadian in twenty was over sixty-five. In 2001, it was one in eight. And by 2026, one in five Canadians will be a senior citizen."

"That's right, Ruth," I said. "I encountered the same statistics in the course of writing my thesis. And projecting ahead even further, by 2040 nearly one-quarter of the Canadian population will be over sixty-five. The only way to mitigate this trend—short of encouraging people to have more babies—is through immigration. The demographic spread in other countries around the world is quite different from that in North America, and many countries have quite young populations. If we can encourage some of these young people to move here, through changes to our immigration policies, that might offset the aging of our population a bit."

"Well, we're already a nation of immigrants," Ruth said. "But this is the first Canadian generation that has not replaced itself. I read an interesting fact lately: by the end of this decade, 100 percent of our population increase will be the result of immigration. And Canadians are now coming from less traditional places. At the turn of the last century, when we had waves of European immigrants, it was easier to assimilate them into the Canadian mosaic. Even if there was a difference in language, there was a constant in religion and culture. As our immigration shifts, we're certainly going to see changes in the values and ideals of our nation."

"That's true," Hazen interrupted. "But why don't you let Meredith finish telling us about her thesis?"

"Sorry, Meredith," Ruth said. "I didn't mean to get side-tracked. It's just that I get so excited when it comes to discussions of changes to society."

"Understood." I grinned at her. "I share some of that excitement." It was clear that the sociologist in Ruth would never retire!

"So, what are the implications for society of this aging population?" Hazen was determined to get us back on track.

"Well, for one thing, we are slowly becoming aware that aging doesn't mean what it once did. The senior years used to be associated with illness and dependency. Today's seniors are, for the most part, healthy and independent. And this will be even more true of tomorrow's seniors. As the National Advisory Council on Aging so aptly points out, social policy must change so that seniors who are in good health can continue to achieve personal and social goals. Seniors are often very active volunteers, for example, and this needs to be encouraged. Boomers already make up 44 percent of Canada's volunteer force, and that will likely increase as they become seniors, especially as they leave the paid labour force. But that's another thing: now that seniors are so healthy, both mentally and physically, there's no need for them to retire at sixty-five. The traditional retirement age is increasingly arbitrary: sixty-five is no longer old! Just look at you guys." I gestured towards Ruth and Hazen. "You are certainly still in the prime of your lives! But in our increasingly knowledge-based society, seniors are going to have to be willing to update their skills to stay active in the labour force. And governments and industries need to be willing to enable their older workers to keep developing their skills, rather than focusing on pushing them out to make way for young people who already have the relevant training. Otherwise, there will soon be a labour shortage, as the young population moving into the labour force isn't anywhere near as large as the generation moving out."

With that, I paused for a sip of wine. I could see the wheels turning in Hazen's and Ruth's heads.

"Those are some intriguing ideas," Ruth said.

"Perhaps a little too heady for a Friday night," Pieter broke in.

"Now, now, Pieter, we don't glaze over when you talk about the wondrous world of bits and bytes," Ruth shot back. "What was your second theme, Meredith?"

I shot Pieter a look. "That women's entry into the work-force not only caused significant changes to the traditional family model, but also led to a dramatic increase in affluence. That leads into my third theme. We are doing very well—possibly too well. I quoted a piece from John Kenneth Galbraith's *The Affluent Society*. I think it goes something like this: 'The poor man has always a precise view of his problem and its remedy: he hasn't enough and he needs more. The rich man can assume or imagine a much greater variety of ills, and he will be correspondingly less certain of their remedies.' Baby boomers seem to have become victims of our affluence—we now have both enough time and enough money to be miserable. This applies across the board for all socio-economic groups. Because many of our material wants have been satisfied, we are suddenly asking, 'Is this all there is?' The answer is, 'Yes—isn't this enough?'"

"That's interesting, Meredith. But it doesn't seem to jibe with all the panic we've heard lately from the media about boomers not having enough money put away to make their retirements comfortable," Hazen said.

"That's true, Hazen. There really is a problem here, and the problem is that boomers tend to live too much in the here and now. When we want something, we go out and get it. Where our parents might have saved for something they needed, we boomers are just as likely to buy it on credit. So we *are* relatively affluent, compared to previous generations, but we're not saving anywhere near enough for the future. This ties back in to life expectancy, which is now almost twenty years for those who have reached sixty-five. Previous generations didn't need to worry about having enough money to last them for twenty years after retirement!"

"Living in the here and now..." Hazen mused. "Yes. That aptly explains the way boomers react to the investment markets too. They have a tendency to chase investments that are hot, and to become overly pessimistic when the markets are down. It's human nature, I guess, but it causes significant damage to the markets."

"Why do I get the feeling you're thinking about me when you say that?" Pieter gave Hazen a wry smile.

"Well, it does tie in to what Jamie was talking about last week when we were playing golf: the importance of having an overall financial plan, and not getting caught up in the day-to-day vagaries of the market. Have you had a chance to talk further with Jamie about your own plan?"

"We've set up a meeting for next week," Pieter responded.

"It's interesting the way everything kind of fits together," Ruth said. "Getting back to Meredith's point about living in the here and now, I've been thinking a lot lately about Stephen Covey's ideas about urgency addiction and the problems it causes in our finances and our lives. Boomers are obsessed with the need to get things done in a hurry. Unfortunately, they've been taught to be impatient."

"I'm afraid we've gotten sidetracked from your thesis again, Meredith," Hazen said.

"Oh, that's okay. Isn't that the point of conversation? It shouldn't just be me spouting my ideas. Discussions are much more interesting."

"Well, Ruth and I will certainly want to read your thesis, Meredith. It sounds like great stuff. How did your advisor react?" Hazen asked.

"I think I passed," I replied.

"I know your advisor well," Ruth said. "Isabel was very impressed with your work. Mature students often do some of the most interesting studies because they bring perspectives and experience with them that younger students simply don't have."

"Speaking of mature writers, we have news to share with you," Hazen said.

Pieter laughed. "We love it when you have an announcement, because the news is always something unexpected."

Ruth smiled and said, "This time we're acting on advice Meredith gave us a few years back."

"My advice?" I was puzzled. I couldn't for the life of me remember what I had suggested.

"We've been letting the idea bubble under the surface

ever since then. We just needed the right time and circumstances in our lives to make it happen," Hazen responded.

"My retirement—or should I say my changing focus—was the catalyst we needed," Ruth said.

"Okay, you two, we're sufficiently curious. What are you talking about?" I said.

"A book," Hazen and Ruth said in unison.

"A book?" Pieter asked.

"You remember the 'boom doctors' thing you suggested several years ago, Meredith?" Hazen continued.

"Oh, yes, I remember now," I replied.

"After we played golf, Pieter, I couldn't get Jamie's notion of the importance of having a plan out of my head. I came home, and Ruth and I were hashing things out, and one thing led to another. We've decided to write the ultimate boomer book."

Ruth went on, "Lately I've been thinking a lot about the fact that the boomers are hitting the halfway marker in their careers and their lives. But the paths of both their careers and their lives are unpredictable because of the changing work patterns we are seeing. There are also likely to be some breakthroughs in health care, and life expectancies are certain to edge up."

"That really ties into the work I did on my thesis," I piped up.

Hazen was getting excited, as he often does. "Think of the issues we will continue to face. Health care, obviously, but also health maintenance and pension concerns. What will the impact be on investment markets, products, the economy, productivity? Important stuff."

"There's another issue that is slowly edging its way into

society," I said. "We are losing our Second World War generation, which means the boomers are having an even larger impact on our values and beliefs."

"We are also losing our connection to the Depression's hold on our thinking as that generation slowly dies," Hazen responded.

"So, when do you plan to start writing this book?" Pieter asked.

"Well, first we have to chart our course and figure out our goals and objectives," Ruth replied.

"So far, we have determined that the book needs to focus equally on the social and financial implications of our changing population structure," Hazen said.

"We feel that your financial life and your actual life are really one and the same," Ruth continued. "We need to know what we are doing, what the world is doing to us and what we *need* to do to finance what we *want* to do."

"Well, there's certainly lots to consider," I said. "I'd love to discuss some of these issues with you."

"Oh, we want you to do more than that," Ruth replied.

"We figured the two of us would need an intermediary," Hazen said. "Someone to keep us balanced and on track, and perhaps to mediate peace agreements if the discussions become too lively. Ruth and I have a problem now that we didn't have before, in that we don't have separate homes. So this research needs to be amicable. And with the experience you've gained with your thesis, we think you'll be the prefect researcher to assist us."

I smiled. "So I get to be chief researcher and peacekeeper."

"That's your precise job description," Ruth replied.

For the rest of the evening, we talked about our families. Hazen and Ruth were genuinely pleased that Dylan was back in town. It's hard on parents when a child moves away, as we were learning for ourselves now that Malcolm was at university—and not even home for the summer.

As the boom doctors prepared to depart, we set up an initial book-planning meeting for the following week. I couldn't wait!

4

You Can't Get There from Here

PIETER

Two weeks had gone by since our golf game, and the day had arrived for Meredith and me to meet with Jamie Arsenault. I was intrigued by the ideas Jamie had introduced on the golf course. To be truthful, I had been very upset the morning of our golf game, and I hadn't found any consolation in the knowledge that many of my cohort are struggling with the same financial issues.

Hazen had introduced us to investing almost a decade ago. We had spoken with friends to get advice on whom to go and see. Eventually, we ended up with one of the large national firms that offer a full range of services. But somehow it hadn't worked out as planned.

There have been successes. We transferred the kids' Canada Savings Bonds into moderate-risk RESPs, which have helped a great deal to offset the cost of Malcolm's university. When Emily heads off in a few years, we'll have a good head start on paying her tuition, and we still have time to top up.

The real disappointment has come in our self-directed

retirement accounts. They have not performed as I expected, and it seems the harder I try, the more I read, the more confused I get. When I make a decision, I'm not sure it's the right thing to do, and I feel like it may make things worse. The advice I've received was well intentioned and reasonable, but even though we laid out a plan, something always throws us off track. Plus, with the markets, there often seems to be too much choice, too many options to pursue. And then there's the constant noise from the media.

Lately, there has been the added pressure of time. And I don't mean I'm too busy to find time to act on investments; more like I'm running out of time to get it right. My crankiness on the course was caused by a feeling similar to the one you get near the end of an exam when you still have lots of work to do and time's running out.

But perhaps this was a chance to make a fresh start. Jamie and I had chatted for a few minutes while setting up a time for the meeting. He was adamant that Meredith attend: "If you're going to get this right, I need both of you to design and buy into this plan."

When we arrived, we were shown into an outside meeting room and offered a coffee. While we were waiting, Andrew Proctor popped in and introduced himself. I remembered that Jamie had mentioned him on the golf course as a senior partner in the firm. Andrew told us that if our preliminary discussions with Jamie worked out, we'd be seeing a lot more of him in the future. Then he ran off to meet with another client. Jamie came in a moment later and said, "Thanks for coming in this morning. I hope you didn't have any trouble parking."

"No, it was fine. Jamie, this is my wife, Meredith," I said.

Jamie extended his hand to greet Meredith. "Let me start by saying that the purpose of this meeting is to flesh out some ideas relating to your financial and overall well-being. It's a time for us to ask some questions of each other and see if we have common ground to continue. This process may lead you to a relationship with our firm, or it may not. If we're successful, what we want to accomplish is an understanding of what you want to do and how you can get there."

Jamie had a way about him that was disarming. He came across as having no agenda, and I sensed a real willingness to try to help us.

"Jamie, obviously this meeting has come about because of our discussion on the golf course a couple of weeks ago. You seemed to know what I was up against and why I was upset," I said.

"When I asked you what you are doing in the market, it was designed to demonstrate how critical it is to have a plan and to be able to articulate the how and why of what you're doing. If the why is important enough, we can design an appropriate how. Your situation, like that of so many other investors, reminds me of that old line 'You can't get there from here.' You can't achieve your goals by following the course of action you have been—you simply won't be able to get where you need to be. You need a road map, a plan, to direct you on how to proceed. We all need to learn how to stop and ask for directions—especially us men!" Jamie grinned. "So why don't you give me an overview of both the good and the bad of what you are currently doing."

"Well, when we got started ten years ago, we were

reasonably well organized," Meredith said, pulling out our financial file.

"Initially, we were pretty good at tracking our expenses, but then we got busy and it just seemed to fall through the cracks," I added.

"That's a very common problem with anything we do: how do you stick to it?" Jamie said.

"We have educational plans for our two children set up. Our son is finishing his BA this year, and our daughter is going into grade ten," Meredith said.

"And those accounts are fine," I said. "We really haven't had any issues; in fact, they've been an enormous help to our cash flow as the costs of university have increased."

"Okay, that's fine," Jamie replied. "How about your investment accounts for your retirement?"

I paused to pull out the statements for our RRSPs. "Okay, here are our statements from the last quarter. We took out a catch-up loan several years ago that allowed us to fully fund our RRSPs. We retired the loan fairly quickly, and the additional capital was well timed, given the uptick in the markets. For a while, we felt flush, and it looked like we were making all the right moves."

Meredith cut in, "Then the stock market started to drop rapidly, and I, for one, felt very vulnerable. It led to some heated debates, particularly when specific stocks just got killed. I think some of Pieter's stress has come from these events."

"We felt vulnerable and suddenly powerless," I continued. "Given my background as an engineer, I want to feel like I understand things, and the markets seemed suddenly to be out of my league."

Jamie grinned at the mention of my engineering background. "Let me start there, Pieter, because your technical predisposition can be a real benefit to solving some of your issues."

"How so?" I asked.

Jamie continued, "Our business model, as I suggested a moment ago, is designed around the importance of a plan. Our engineering clients understand this instinctively. It goes to their basic training and beliefs. Do you know the history behind the iron ring on your little finger?"

"Of course," I responded. "Every engineer that wears the ring has gone through the Ritual of the Calling that started back in the 1920s. It symbolizes that we are part of the engineering profession and hold ourselves to very high standards."

"But what's the significance of the ring, Pieter?" Jamie asked.

"Well, the original rings were made from the iron of a bridge that collapsed near Quebec City, killing a lot of people," I responded. "An inquiry revealed that the disaster was the result of errors made by the bridge's engineers. Thus, the ring is meant to remind us that, although we have pride in our profession, we must also have humility."

"All this time I've seen you wearing your ring, and I never knew the significance," Meredith said.

"It's all about process," Jamie responded. "The iron reminds engineers that there is only one way to do things. There can be no shortcuts, no quick fixes. They have to adhere to the principles that govern the laws of engineering, or disasters will happen. The investment market is no different. If you don't follow a specific process, the result could be financial disaster."

"I've never thought about it that way," I responded. "By the way, they make the rings out of nickel now so they won't rust."

Jamie shuffled papers for a moment. "I joked about the members of your profession the other day, but in fact engineers are our best clients. They instinctively crave process because of their training. Once we establish a process for your financial management, I think you will discover that many of your frustrations will disappear."

"What exactly do you mean by 'process'?" Meredith asked.

"Good question. I mean a very specific list of guidelines that govern your investments, including a solid financial plan, a knowledge of your risk tolerance, and an asset mix that suits both those criteria. If you are guided by process, you won't make the mistake of chasing the markets, looking for the hot 'investment du jour.' There is a lot of ready-shoot-aim going on in the markets. I see this, by the way, mostly with my male clients."

Meredith smiled.

"Men tend to put the cart ahead of the horse," he continued. "Before you can invest, you need a financial plan. No self-respecting businessperson would try to run a business without a plan, and neither should investors. Without a plan, we are subject to the vagaries of the market and the pitfalls of human nature. And I suggest a very specific, well-thought-out written document that lists priorities, goals and objectives. I say 'written' because by writing our plan down we make a covenant with ourselves, and it's easier to stay focused. Once your plan is laid out, we'll use the different asset classes—cash, real estate, stocks and bonds—simply as a means to an end."

"How does the plan take shape?" I asked.

"We derive your financial plan out of a needs-and-priorities analysis. It's all about technique." Jamie paused for a moment, as if he had suddenly thought of something. "I saw something the other night on the golf channel that may strike a chord with you, Pieter. I was up at two in the morning walking with my four-month-old daughter. You may recall those days."

Meredith and I both smiled.

"We remember them well," Meredith replied.

"Well, I tune in to the golf channel when I'm up late, and they had a pro on talking about setup." Meredith looked blank, so Jamie added, "Sorry, Meredith, setup is how you line up in front of the ball. His point was that more than 90 percent of golfers have mis-hit the ball before they even make contact because their setup is wrong. They only discover the problem after they hit the ball and it flies into the woods."

"That sounds familiar," I said.

"His suggestion was to seek help, work to have the proper setup and stance, and practise like crazy so that your swing action becomes repeatable and consistent," Jamie continued. "We need to take the same approach to the markets."

"I guess the real key is getting a good coach," I suggested.

"Of course. It's a mistake to go to a range and endlessly hit the wrong way. You may improve eventually, but seeking help would be easier and would save an enormous amount of time and effort," Jamie said.

Meredith, as much as she found golf pointless, seemed to

be following along. "So, how do we translate that to our situation?" she asked.

"We start from the beginning. When I first started in this business, my dad gave me a bunch of audiotapes from some of the well-known thinkers in the area of self-improvement. It's amazing how relevant some of the non-financial stuff is," Jamie said.

"I've always found that stuff a little hokey," I responded.

"Perhaps, but it works. 'Start with the end in mind.' That's Stephen Covey's second habit of highly effective people. You need to figure out what you want your future to look like. What are your dreams, your goals? There are a great many benefits to planning for the future in this way, not the least of which is communication between the two of you on what you expect the future to hold. You may find that you have completely different ideas about this, but by beginning to talk about the future now you'll have a chance to resolve any issues, short- or long-term. Once you know what your goals are, you can create a plan that will enable you to achieve them. Another self-help guru, Tony Robbins, talks a lot about having a written plan that articulates not only your financial goals but also your family, career, spiritual and relationship goals. He introduced me to the idea of having a compelling future. Extremely powerful stuff: if you have goals, plan them out, and prioritize them, you can't miss."

"And you've seen this work for your clients?" Meredith asked.

"Of course, because they figured out what to ask for. Remember, ask and you shall receive. But be careful what you ask for. Use your wishes wisely," Jamie concluded.

"How did they figure out which of their goals and dreams were wise ones?" I asked.

"You start on a long journey by taking the first step," Jamie replied. "Start discussing a life plan that details what you and Meredith want to do in the future. With your younger child heading off to college in a few years, you're about to enter the next phase in your life. Your life plan will help us with the financial planning we do for you."

"So you're not involved in the life-planning aspects, per se?" Meredith asked.

"That part's really up to you. I can't tell you how your life should unfold. I'm certainly interested in your dreams and aspirations, but it's your life—you plan it. We handle the financial aspects—the nuts and bolts that flow from your future plan—and around this we determine investment policy," Jamie replied.

"Okay, so the first step is for us to create a life plan, and from that you'll help us create a financial plan, is that right?" I asked.

"That's right. I have a bunch of reference material for you to review and discuss with each other."

"So, we have some homework to wade through," Meredith said.

Jamie nodded. "There's quite a bit of front-end work for you two. As well as the reference material, I am going to give you a financial planning workbook and a questionnaire. If you were a business, the workbook would be your balance sheet, income statement and business plan all rolled into one. It looks at all cash-flow issues and prioritizes debt and repayment issues. It also looks at assets and how they are allocated to maximize outcomes."

"And what's the purpose of the questionnaire?" I asked.

"It's designed to give us a basic assessment of your attitudes towards risk and also to help you prioritize your goals and objectives. These are the inputs we use. Some are more scientific, and some are much more subjective."

"What do the outputs look like?" Meredith asked.

"I was hoping you'd ask. The output is a very specific plan that guides your actions. It determines what you need to do, and it is articulated in an investment policy statement. This statement reviews your risk tolerance, which leads to your asset mix, which leads to your execution of your investment. In the future, Pieter, if someone asks you, 'What are you doing in the market?' I hope you respond, 'That's not the point. I use the market as a means to an end, and my involvement is governed by my investment policy statement.' That ought to confuse them." Jamie took a long breath.

"But in the end this process actually works?" I asked.

"Andrew and I have been through this so many times now that we *know* it works," Jamie said. "The interesting thing is, we see similar trends develop in all of our successful clients."

"When you say it that way, it sounds as though not all of your clients *are* successful," Meredith observed.

Jamie nodded his head. "There are some that struggle with change; it's inevitable that it's not for everyone."

"But there are common threads among your clients who are successful?" Meredith asked.

"I call what they have in common 'the pillars of wealth,'" Jamie replied. "We have a preconceived idea of what wealth looks like. Generally, a lot of money. But I think wealth is more specific, and that's where our plan leads us."

"How many of these 'pillars of wealth' are there?" Meredith asked.

"Four," Jamie replied. "Now, keep in mind that this is relative wealth I am speaking of. The successful investors are people who are generally very comfortable with their current and future situations. First, they are debt-free. Second, they live within their means. That is not to say they are frugal, necessarily; they just have a good grasp of what sustainable expenditure levels look like. Third, they have developed—often by themselves—a reasonable risk tolerance and an appropriate asset mix, and have funded it and stuck with it. And last, they have a pension that gives them a great sense of stability."

Meredith had been taking notes, but now she looked up. I knew she was thinking what I was thinking. Almost in unison, we said, "But we don't have a pension."

Jamie nodded. "Precisely. So we better get busy and create one for you. And the first step is for you folks to go home and discuss your life plan."

"I take it we're not going to get to what I should be doing in the market today?" I asked with a grin.

"Not a chance. But when I'm through with you, you'll never have to be concerned about the market again," Jamie replied.

"You can't imagine what a relief that would be," Meredith said.

We thanked Jamie for his time. He reminded us that our talks were preliminary and that we should think about whether we feel the process he proposed is a good fit for us. "The approach is involved," he said, "and all parties need to be engaged to secure the desired end result. Many people are looking for a simpler approach; if that's true of you, I would encourage you to acknowledge it before we go any further. In the meantime, please feel free to call me if there's anything you need clarified."

With that, we headed out the door with our homework, ready to talk about our life plan.

5
Trust Yourself

MEREDITH

"Hey, are you back here?" I called, as I walked into Ruth and Hazen's back garden. There's nothing worse than walking in on people unexpectedly and shocking the bejesus out of them. Since they'd moved in together five years ago—in wedded bliss—Ruth and Hazen had become quite the pair of lovebirds. I didn't want to walk in on a romantic moment in their secluded backyard.

"Meredith, is that you?" I heard Ruth's voice. I looked around the garden but couldn't see her. She could obviously see me, trying to find her: I could hear her soft chuckling. But where the heck...?

"Look up, way up," she said, in a fine imitation of the Friendly Giant of CBC fame. There she was, perched on the roof of her house.

"What are you doing up there?"

"I'm creating a trellis for a clematis vine to climb this wall," she replied. "I want it to grow to the rooftop within a year or two, so I'm getting ready for it now. You know me. I always have a long-term plan. I want to add a burst of colour to this garden, and this clematis has the most gorgeous deep pink flowers."

"How did you get up there?"

"I crawled out one of the bedroom windows," she replied. The house had a one-storey addition in the back, and by opening one of the second-storey windows Ruth had clambered onto the lower roof of the addition. "Like I say, I've always got a plan. Wait a minute, I'll be right down, and I'll put on a pot of tea on my way out to the garden."

As I waited, I took a quick tour of Ruth and Hazen's garden. They had transformed this small urban space into a quiet, relaxing sanctuary with nothing more than a few plants, some basic lawn furniture, a gurgling fountain (now that was new; I hadn't seen it before), a sound plan for what they wanted their garden to be, and good taste.

It felt good to relax on a Saturday morning. The past few months had been stressful, tiring and very full. I'd been struggling to finish my master's thesis. Pieter had been in a funk—worried, as always, about our family's finances and the state of our investments. Malcolm had survived his first year at university, although there were some anxious phone calls around final exams. And I'd been driving Emily all over town, helping her drop off her résumés. She was dead keen to find her first summer job, but the perfect job was proving elusive for our high-school girl. She was unhappy and, as anyone who's lived with a teenage girl knows, when she's unhappy, so are you. So it felt good to be in this serene, peaceful garden, with a couple of minutes to ponder.

Ruth burst into my pensive world, bustling out the back door. "Kettle's on," she said, giving me a warm hug. "What brings you here on a Saturday morning?"

"I'm returning the book you lent me and bringing along

another that might interest you. And I thought we might start talking about our game plan for your book."

"Hazen's down at Hank's HouseCare, so perhaps we should wait for him before we talk about our plans. But there's no reason we can't have a good chat!" Ruth said. "Did you like *The Progress Paradox?*"

The day after our barbecue dinner, Ruth had turned up at my door, excited about a book she'd discovered, *The Progress Paradox*. She'd loaned it to me, extracting the promise that we'd discuss it when I'd finished. "It's really all old news, and I know we've talked about this before," she'd said of the book. "But the author, Gregg Easterbrook, makes his argument so well. It's about how life in Western countries has improved so dramatically over the past century, and yet people are no more happy than in previous generations. Hey, I could have told you that years ago—but not nearly so eloquently as Easterbrook."

Ruth then launched into a recollection of her Uncle Jack, a rabbi in Montreal and a force in Ruth's spiritual life. She often quotes him when she talks of life's big lessons. "Uncle Jack always said, 'There must be more to life than having everything.' It was his way of saying that material stuff isn't what feeds the soul. Things—even lots of wonderful things—do not make you content with what life has to offer. The boomers are finding out the hard way that the popular nineties notion 'He who dies with the most toys wins' couldn't be more false."

"So what does feed the soul? What will make me—and other boomers like me—content?" I asked at the time.

"Read the book and we'll talk," she'd said, pressing *The Progress Paradox* into my hands.

That was two weeks ago. School was finally finished, and I had some time to read things other than school textbooks. Now I was ready to talk.

I had brought along another book I'd discovered in the interim—a perfect follow-up to *The Progress Paradox*, I thought. This one, *The Paradox of Choice* by Barry Schwartz, is all about choice overload. Too many choices in life translate into anxiety and unhappiness. At least, that's the thesis of the book. I wanted to hear what my wise friend Ruth might have to say about that.

"Before we start talking about the human condition, I want to talk about your condition," I began. "Is it a good idea for you to be climbing around on your roof with no one around to keep an eye on you?"

"So you're telling me I'm too old for high places?" Ruth shot back.

"In a word, yes."

"Haven't you noticed? I'm a GOTY. You don't need to worry about people like us." She laughed.

"Okay—what's a GOTY?" I could see she was trying to divert the conversation, and I was going to get nowhere with my suggestion that she keep her feet firmly planted on the ground.

"Getting Older, Thinking Younger. This should interest you, as a scholar focused on the aging population. Research shows that older people in North America and Europe have never been happier. They're in fine form: 75 percent say they have a good attitude about their lives. Sixty is the new forty. I'll tell you, I feel like I'm forty. I certainly don't feel old. Like my Uncle Jack always said, 'To me, old age is always fifteen years older than I am.'"

I had to admit, Ruth is in great shape for a woman in her sixties.

"But you should know all this," she said. *"The Progress Paradox* says that the older you are, the happier you are. I can tell you that my sense of well-being has increased over the years."

"Well, I'm a bit envious," I replied.

Now that I had my master's, I wasn't quite sure what my career path might be. That was one of the reasons I was so delighted when Ruth and Hazen offered me the job working on their book. It would allow me to put off taking a good, hard look at my long-term plan. I wasn't certain where I was headed, or even where I wanted to head.

I knew I wasn't alone in my career uncertainty. For my thesis, I had relied on research from Carleton University's Sprott School of Business. That work clearly reveals that what people look for in a career depends on their age. Those born before 1945—the Silent Generation—want to leave a legacy. The Baby Bust Generation, or Generation Xers, born between 1966 and 1979, are looking for intellectually stimulating work. Those born after 1980—the Millennials—want money and fun. But it seems to me that boomers place the heaviest personal demands on the work world—they want the perfect balance of work and life. Work for them (or should I say "us"?) must be in accord with their morals, lifestyles and values. Boomers are a demanding lot, as usual. And I am a classic boomer. Now I wondered if I would ever find the perfect career.

Once again, Ruth jolted me out of my thoughts. "Come into the kitchen while I make the tea, and let's talk about your generation and its unhappy state."

"It's funny. My rational mind knows that I'm programmed to feel anxiety about the future, but my emotions can still take me on a wild roller-coaster ride, worrying about what lies ahead," I said, as we walked into the house.

"Yes, Easterbrook discusses that extensively in *The Progress Paradox*—the fact that evolution has programmed us to fear the worst. No matter how good we have it, we'll find something to complain about, worry about or feel bad about." Ruth poured hot water into the teapot. "But, as I said when I lent you the book, that thought is not new. Years ago, Adlai Stevenson said, 'The human race has improved everything except the human race.'"

"In fact, sometimes I think the human race goes out of its way to diminish the human race," I replied.

"That's an interesting comment. What do you mean?" Ruth asked, loading cups and some delicious-looking biscuits onto a tray.

"CNN is a perfect example of a force that reduces us. That network is 24/7, wall-to-wall hysteria. Everything from 'Man Beheaded in Iraq' to 'Little Bobby's Trapped in a Well' is presented at a fever pitch, with little or no analysis and no effort to put small issues into the big context of the world. Again, the rational mind knows the sky isn't falling. But if you bought into the negative CNN view, your emotional mind would believe that things are very bad and getting worse for the human race."

"I think Easterbrook called it 'amplified anxiety' in his book," Ruth answered, ushering me back into the garden. "We get carried away worrying about small risks. Easterbrook maintains that it's a phenomenon of a modern, prosperous society meeting the basic nature of the human race. Substantial risks like wars, plagues and famines aren't happening on this continent. But we have the knowledge and leisure to detect small risks. We have to worry about something, and that explains why CNN goes on for days about a poor child who's fallen down a well."

"Yeah. I have to say, I watched that coverage, and I've never worried about either Malcolm or Emily ending up at the bottom of a well. That's one of my life's smallest concerns," I said.

We settled into Ruth's comfortable garden chairs.

"It's human nature to be fearful. It kept early man watchful, aware and safe from lions, tigers or bears," she said, pouring the tea and putting the drop of milk she knew I liked into my cup. "'We have nothing to fear but fear itself.' Do you know who said that?" she asked.

"I've certainly heard that saying, but I don't have a clue who came up with it."

"Franklin Delano Roosevelt. He said it during his inaugural address in 1933, when he was first elected president. Now, that was a time when people actually had something to worry about—it was the early years of the Great Depression. Many people had lost everything they owned. But FDR was before his time. During that same speech, he reminded Americans that, even though times were tough, the difficulties concerned only material things. He told listeners that the generations that preceded them had faced much tougher times and that, in 1933, everyone still had much to be thankful for. In that same speech, he also said, 'Happiness lies not in the mere possession of money; it lies in the joy of achievement, in the thrill of creative effort.'"

"Boy, you sure do like FDR. I'm impressed that you can quote him like that," I said.

"I haven't told Hazen yet, but in our book I want to focus on the theme of creating a vision for the future—something FDR firmly believed both individuals and nations should do. To my way of thinking, a vision is the first step in developing a long-term plan, and I feel everyone should spend some time thinking about creating their life plan. As part of my research for the book, I've spent some time in the past couple of days reading and rereading FDR's speech. It's memorable. People could really speak well and powerfully back then."

"It's funny you should mention life plans. Pieter and I met with Jamie the other day, and he set us to the task of creating a life plan."

"That's terrific!" Ruth said. "That should help lessen your anxiety about the future."

"I certainly hope so," I said. "What a relief that would be. But I'm glad you raised the issue of being thankful for what you've got. FDR was reminding an entire country to be grateful, and you've just reminded me I should count my blessings," I said. "It's easy to forget when you're busy with school, kids, mortgage payments, work, grocery shopping, dog walking. You know the drill."

"I sure do. When Dylan was young, I was working so hard to get tenure at the university, I didn't have a spare minute to call my own," Ruth mused. "It's easy to get bogged down in life. That's why FDR was so ahead of the curve in his call for Americans to be grateful for what they had, despite being mired in the depths of the Depression."

"What do you mean by 'ahead of the curve'?"

"Easterbrook wrote about the developing field of 'positive psychology' in *The Progress Paradox*," Ruth said.

"Yes, I remember. People who learn to be grateful and forgiving end up being healthier and happier than grumps who take a negative view of things."

"Well, FDR knew, back in 1933, that a positive attitude was one of the key things necessary to pull the U.S. out of the Depression. Again, positive psychology is nothing new. Like Uncle Jack used to say, 'Life is a tragedy full of joy.' Tough times will come your way during your lifetime—you can be sure of that. But there will be lots of good times too. Don't get mired in cynicism, keep yourself thankful, and you'll be happier."

"Yeah, well, that's easier said than done," I replied.

"You're in quite a mood for a sunny Saturday morning."

"As I said, I know I have lots to be grateful for: my kids are healthy, I have a strong marriage, I have a good education. But it can be hard to keep all the good things uppermost in my mind when I'm facing challenges, particularly of the financial variety."

"Nobody said life would be easy, but I'm around to remind you that positive thinking is good for you—your body and your soul. I'll be your own personal Dalai Lama. You remember that I went to see him when he was in Ottawa?"

I nodded in reply. I knew how moved Ruth had been by the comments of the man who called himself "a simple monk from Tibet."

"The Dalai Lama spoke of facing tough times in life. You can either lose hope or use the challenge to find inner strength. The choice is yours. Simple. I will keep reminding you to find your inner strength, to keep your eyes on the future and to trust," she said.

"Trust? Trust who? Trust what?"

"Simple—yourself. Stay the course and keep yourself thankful for what life has to offer you. You can't control your future, but through your vision and your plans you can sure change your approach to what lies in store for you and your family."

"Cripes! My family! I forgot all about them, sitting here, drinking tea. It's nearly ten! I've got to get home to drive Emily to a job interview. She'll kill me if I'm not on time. Really, I've got to run. Here," I said, handing her a plastic shopping bag with the two books I'd brought over. "One is yours, the other is *The Paradox of Choice* by Barry Schwartz. Knowing you, I bet you'll have finished it by the next time I see you. I'll be back in a couple of days to finish this conversation. Thanks for the tea!"

I left Ruth smiling and shaking her head, quietly sipping her cup of tea. I charged out of the garden and ran down the street. I was feeling stressed—Emily was waiting—but somehow things didn't seem nearly as serious as when I'd entered Ruth's secret garden.

6

The Nature of Human Nature

HAZEN

True to his word, Jamie had asked his senior partner, Andrew Proctor, to give me a call. We shared at least one thing in common: Andrew liked to play golf first thing in the morning. We had arranged to play on Tuesday of the following week.

Ruth and I were starting to have preliminary discussions on the nature and direction of the research for our book. I'm not sure why, but when ideas start to percolate they lead to even more ideas, and you can never tell what's going to pop up next.

Maybe it's always been this way, but it seems to me that a great deal has been going on in the world lately. The advent of twenty-four-hour news probably contributes to this perception: there's not necessarily more going on, it's just that we now hear more about events around the world. Yet I'm certain more news has not led to more social stability for anyone.

As we headed into the new millennium, it struck me as unusual that during the run-up to Y2K we also had an extraordinary run-up in the markets. Alan Greenspan described this as "irrational exuberance" but, in reality, it was your basic, everyday, run-of-the-mill bubble. It's how people react that's the key. In his famous book, *Extraordinary Popular Delusions and the Madness of Crowds*, Charles MacKay outlines some historical examples of irrational behaviour: Tulipmania, the South Sea Bubble. We seem to have a habit of getting carried away. The baby boomers came into their formative investing years in the midst of the "irrational exuberance" in the markets. Actually, it would be reasonable to say they contributed to this bubble. And since then, we seem to have lurched from one problem to the next. The tech bubble burst, then came the scandals of corporate malfeasance. The United States headed off to remake Iraq, whether the Iraqis wanted help or not. And throughout it all, CNN was there to keep us updated. We certainly are living in interesting times.

And then Jamie asked that simple question of Pieter on the golf course, and it's been running through my head ever since. Sometimes the simplest observations are the best. Perhaps we have lost focus because we are constantly bombarded with information. Jamie's right: we need to get back to basics. That brings me back to the David Foot–Michael Adams debate: How predictable are the baby boomers? What does the future hold for them and the economy? How will their retirement unfold, and what impact will an aging population have on our nation?

Important questions. I was keen to meet with Andrew and get his take on some of these issues.

Tuesday finally rolled around, and I was off to the golf course. When you have the first tee time, it's reasonably easy to spot a playing partner you've never met. As I pulled into the parking lot, a solitary figure was rolling putts on the practice green. I got out of my car and walked over.

"I suspect you're Andrew Proctor," I said, sticking out my hand. He looked vaguely familiar: I was sure I had seen him around the club.

"Hazen! It's great to finally meet you," he responded. "I've followed your work for some time, especially since Jamie came to work for us. He's very fond of you."

I smiled. "It's a great pleasure to see him doing so well."

"He arrived at a perfect time to join our team," Andrew replied. "A significant shift is taking place in our industry, and it's the younger professionals who are leading the way."

Andrew had piqued my interest. I was keenly interested in knowing how younger advisors were changing the industry, so I kept his comment in the back of my mind when Andrew changed the subject on our way to the first tee.

"Early-morning golf is one of life's interesting trade-offs, especially as you get older," Andrew said. "You get to play a nice fast-paced game; unfortunately, the stiffness in your body takes a few holes to work out."

I laughed. "You should try it when you're my age. All those foolish activities you did in your youth come back to haunt you."

"The sounds and smells are worth it, though. The world gets noisier later in the day, and you can't beat the fresh-cut, wet grass smell in the morning. If it costs you a few strokes here and there, I'm certain it's worth it. A little like life, I suspect. Things just seem to work out better when we keep them simple," Andrew replied.

We hit our drives. Andrew's ball sailed down the middle,

but I was forced to implement the "hit until you're happy" rule off the first tee. My first drive sliced out onto a road that was inconveniently located beside the fairway—have to keep the morning drivers on their toes as they drive by! My second attempt was more reasonable, and we were off.

"So, how are young professionals leading the way in your business these days?" I asked, encouraging Andrew to elaborate on his earlier comment. We continued down the fairway, hitting our shots with little trouble.

Andrew smiled. "Well, you can never underestimate a little experience in any profession, so I'm not completely obsolete. But young people do bring a different perspective with them. The traditional methods have not worked for many investors, and young professionals like Jamie are not wedded to these methods. They have new, fresh ideas."

"We discussed some of those ideas with Jamie on this very course a few weeks ago."

"I heard he had an interesting discussion with your friend. Pieter and Meredith came in to see Jamie the other day, and I met them briefly then," Andrew replied.

"Jamie got Pieter's attention by asking him what he was doing in the market. It was interesting to observe Pieter's struggle to understand the question and come up with a response."

"Precisely the problem with investors today: with all due respect, many don't have a notion of what they're doing or where they're going."

We headed off to different sides of the fairway to hit our next shots. Miraculously, we both hit reasonable wedge shots and landed on the green. Andrew putted out in two, and I stickhandled around the green for a bogey—

no point in counting my miscue on the tee. We headed to the next tee.

"An opening par. You're not a sandbagger by any chance, are you?" I asked Andrew, having a little fun with him.

"The true nature of my golf game will become apparent soon enough." He smiled.

We headed down the next fairway and the discussion continued. As usual, I had a dozen ideas racing around in my head. "So why do some investors have such a hard time in the markets?" I asked. "It was always my contention that the baby boomers would affect the markets the same way they hit the schools and real estate and every other commodity that has crossed their paths."

"I know your theory. I've read a couple of your articles on the boomers' expected impact on the markets," Andrew replied.

"So what went wrong?" I asked.

"Nothing, really. They showed up, just as you predicted. But the investment markets are different from other markets, and when they start to go down, a lack of understanding can become obvious in a hurry."

"And by 'a lack of understanding' you mean what?"

"Well, the explanation is a little long winded, so let's putt out and I'll give you my sermon on the next tee."

When we got to the next tee box, Andrew started in. "You were quite right in your contention that the baby boomers would come to the market. They have come in droves. We thought we were being very clever in developing self-directed accounts just as the boomers hit their formative investing years. We opened up the markets and encouraged our largest generation to self-direct and take control of their economic future. Unfortunately, for many of these investors, this empowerment has turned out to be a bad idea. Investing is a lot like golf: both are tougher than they look."

"Let me guess: the unfettered access is too much for many investors to handle."

Andrew nodded. "I always think of the scene between Jack Nicholson and Tom Cruise in the movie *A Few Good Men*. Cruise, the lawyer, shouts at Nicholson, the hardened career Marine, 'I want the truth!' Nicholson responds, 'You can't handle the truth!' We urged this generation to get involved in the markets and said, 'Go ahead, make your fortune.' Well, it turns out many investors can't handle the volatility, and they are often much too short-term in their focus. The markets have a bad habit of moving up and down quite rapidly and unpredictably. Investors need to understand this and learn to go with the ebb and flow of the markets."

"So their lack of process was the problem?"

"It's worse than that. In many cases, self-directed accounts just aren't compatible with human nature. It can be a recipe for disaster."

"Yes, Jamie emphasized that too. But I'd like to hear your take on how human nature hinders self-direction. Of all the things Jamie mentioned, I think this notion fascinated me the most. I thought unfettered access was a good thing."

"Well, first of all, I don't think the boomers understand how the markets work," Andrew continued. "I once heard a speaker talk about the common lament that it's difficult for most people to remember names. He says it's not that we forget the name of a person we have just met. It's that we never knew it to begin with. You can't forget what you never knew."

"I'm not sure I follow."

"When we meet someone for the first time, we often don't concentrate on his or her name. Then we realize moments later that we've forgotten it. We think it's memory, but it's not. We failed to make a mental note when we heard the name, so we never actually knew it. It's our technique that's rotten, not our memory. If we had a system in place for learning a person's name when we first heard it, we wouldn't be apt to forget it. When you shake someone's hand, for example, repeat his or her name or, if it's unusual, ask how it's spelled. Then, at least, your memory has a fighting chance."

"And the same principle holds for successful investing?"

"Yes. Because of a lack of process, investors fall back on gut instinct, or sometimes a hunch or a tip," Andrew replied. "We professionals allow investors to self-direct— and often in a seat-of-the-pants fashion. They go out and do battle with a very complex economic system, often with no more information than the fact that their neighbour or Uncle Sid thought an investment was a good idea. And for long periods—as long as markets are favourable—everything works out just fine. Then the rough market rears its ugly head, as we know it will, and suddenly Uncle Sid doesn't seem so smart."

"And human nature is a big part of the problem."

"Sure is. As the nineties rolled along, more and more Canadians felt like they were missing out on a great opportunity. Many novices flooded the markets and thought they had it figured out. But our ability to think often gets us in trouble. Research scientists at Dartmouth College ran a very interesting test comparing humans and lab rats."

"I sense a punchline coming."

"Indeed. The outcome was very instructive," Andrew continued. "A red light and a green light were placed at opposite ends of a rat's cage. The red light was set to turn on 80 percent of the time, and the green light 20 percent, in a random sequence. When the rat guessed correctly which light would turn on next, and pressed the button below it, he received a food reward. When he guessed incorrectly, he received an unpleasant stimulus."

"The rat got zapped," I said.

"Precisely. It didn't take the rat very long to determine that his best bet was to push the button below the red light every time."

"Rats learn very quickly," I concluded.

"Apparently every rat tested."

"And the humans?"

"Well, they weren't wired, but they were told that the red and green lights would turn on in the same 80:20 ratio and were asked to guess which light would come on next. They were also told that the lights would come on randomly. There was no pattern."

"And how did they fare?"

"No matter how adamantly the testers insisted there was no pattern, most of the subjects believed there was one and tried to figure it out. Interestingly, although the subjects didn't keep count, they tended to push red about 80 percent of the time. Now, on average, this strategy led to a 68-percent success rate—they guessed correctly 80 percent of the time on red and 20 percent of the time on green. The rats, on the other hand, by using what the scientists call a 'maximizing' strategy and pressing only red, scored 80 percent. The rats were better at picking random outcomes because they didn't think. They could be trained to do a specific task, whereas we humans have to use our large brains to reason things out." Andrew smiled.

"We just can't help ourselves."

"Apparently not."

"So how do these tests relate to investing? Something to do with the randomness of the markets, I take it."

"Exactly," Andrew said. "Ernie Ankrim, the chief investment strategist of the Frank Russell Company in the U.S., used this research to back up his hypothesis that investors sabotage themselves when they try to predict the future of the markets. The human need to find patterns in randomness causes us to make bad choices in search of the next big payoff. He emphasized that a long-term strategy was the way to go: like the rats, we need to learn to maximize our chances of getting the best results. We need to fight our human nature and become more like those lab rats!"

"So what can the investment industry do to help us be more like rats?" I asked.

"First, we need to help investors recognize what they're up against. As an industry, we've done a fabulous job over the past twenty years of bringing our largest generation to the markets. We've focused them on the importance of saving for retirement. Where we've done less well is in educating them in the ways of the market. They need to understand the volatility; they need to know how the market fits into their overall asset mix; and they need to know how the investment market and other assets fit into their financial plan. Like the rats, they can maximize outcomes by sticking to the plan."

"And an understanding of investing is even more important as they get older."

"To them, but also to the markets. If we professionals don't take the time now to make investors understand the process, the markets themselves are going to be in trouble."

I had become so caught up in our chat that I was surprised to see we were at the halfway snack shack. I have a little motivational game I play: if I score under 50 in the first nine, I get a chocolate chip muffin; if I play poorly, a bran muffin. It's a win-win proposition. Today, I had opened the first nine with an even 52. Shooting my age was impossible, so I resigned myself to a healthy dose of bran.

After a quick snack break, we teed off for the second nine and our engaging conversation continued.

"So you think the markets could be in trouble as the boomers age?" I asked.

"It's hard to tell," Andrew replied. "What worries me is that, as the boomers get older, they won't have a process in place that will help them make wise financial moves in the context of their risk issues and their recommended asset mix. It's one thing not to know what you're doing when you're young. If that persists into your retirement years, panic can set in quickly. Jamie feels that a lack of process is the main source of your friend Pieter's anxiety. I'm his age. I know where he's coming from. All of a sudden, retirement is getting closer."

"And because there are so many boomers, the risk to the markets is magnified," I put in. "When they left the school system, we suddenly had too many schools. If they get spooked by the markets as they age, it will be everyone's problem."

"Sure, it's a huge cohort with very high participation rates. If they are properly advised and invested, there will be a happy ending for both individual investors and the market. But if we professionals can't reach enough of these investors and help them develop their understanding and knowledge of the markets, there could be a lot of bad news for the industry."

We arrived at a very tricky short par three. In my opinion, it's really the shortest par five in the world. The green is ridiculously fast, and it's not uncommon to watch your putt roll past the hole and off the green. Andrew tapped in for a bogey, which he seemed quite happy about. I shot a five, which was fine, given that this hole has driven me crazy since I joined the club.

As we headed up the next fairway, Andrew made an interesting observation. "If we could only get boomers to understand how the markets fit in with their other assets. The financial world is like a big puzzle, and all the pieces fit together."

"If they could relate their stocks to their real estate, for example, they'd be better off?"

"Exactly. I have a lot of ideas about real estate, but I think that discussion is best left for another day. Suffice it to say that if investors could manage their equity as they manage their real estate, we'd all be a lot better off."

"These two assets are very closely related," I said.

"Clearly. They are both tied to the health of our economy. There's a question I like to ask my clients because it's a perfect notional mindset for the markets: If you were to buy property somewhere, would you be more concerned about the climate or the weather?"

"Definitely the climate," I responded.

"Exactly. Who cares about the weather? The climate tells us what to expect year to year over the long term."

"I gather investors worry too much about market 'weather.'"

"They sure do. If you aren't retiring for years, don't get worked up about the weather. Unfortunately, thanks to the media, investors often think they see a hurricane coming in the markets. Many investors are confused about the difference between risk and volatility."

"I would think the average investor believes the two to be the same thing."

"They do, and they're not. The markets carry a great deal of volatility, but over the long run very little risk. In fact, I could make a compelling argument that the true risk lies in *not* investing in the market," Andrew said.

"Investors need to gain understanding and get over their apprehension."

"They need to have a better idea of what they are trying to get done and, most important, what they're up against. And yes, they need to get over their fear. One of my favourite quotes is from Jeremy Siegel's *Stocks for the Long Run*. It goes, 'Fear has a greater grasp on human action than does the impressive weight of historical evidence.'"

"It's the old fear-and-greed tug-of-war on human action, or lack of action," I replied. "That's really the issue, isn't it—raw human emotions. I've always felt that fear and greed are just the opposite extremes of the same spectrum. One holds you back, and one pushes you forward, but they can both lead to bad decisions. That gets us back to your argument about human nature: people tend to get too greedy when there's a bull market, and too fearful when there's a bear market."

"Absolutely," Andrew said. "Part of the problem is that investors lack patience. People are willing to hold on to a home for many, many years, and that almost always results in a positive outcome. But the average holding period for a mutual fund now is less than two years. There's a Warren Buffett line I love because it demonstrates how out of touch some investors are: 'I like to own stocks that if they stopped trading for three years it wouldn't bother me.' Most investors would flip after the first three minutes."

We both had a good laugh and finished up our putts on the seventeenth. We headed for the last hole, and I couldn't resist asking Andrew a few final questions.

"How do we get the boomers focused on process so that markets will continue to be stable in the future?"

"Well, let me draw on one of your own ideas: quantity versus quality," Andrew replied.

"I used to spend a great deal of time on that theme when talking to companies about product development." My idea was that, as we age, our focus switches from quantity needs to quality needs. It's only natural: as you get older, you want a better suit or car or house. "Do you believe the boomers are headed towards their quality investing years?"

"I do. And it's now critical to understand this notion in the investment world. The boomers used to throw money into a retirement plan and grab a stock or a fund or a bond, and they didn't focus too much on the mix. That was fine; they needed to start. Now they need to become very specific. They need to shift to quality stocks, and they need to diversify. It's a new take on your old theme, Hazen. They're going to be increasing their quantity as they age, but what they really need to do is focus on quality. To do this, they need a plan, and they need to stick with it and be patient. Charles Ellis talks about this in one of the consummate investment bibles, *Winning the Loser's Game*. Asset mix is king. Know your time frame, and for goodness' sake don't spend all your time trying to out-think the market. You can't beat yourself."

"And now for the $64,000 question: How do you get the boomers to stick to it?" I asked.

"You set them up with an investment policy when they start," he responded. "You attempt to rein them in. You coach them as often as they will tolerate it. You remind them of process when they head off in the wrong direction. You try to help them understand what they're doing. I've always loved the line 'It's not what happens to you, it's what you do about it.' In the end, though, it's a constant struggle, just as life is sometimes. I'd love to tell you that all of my clients stick to their plan, but they don't. As I've said before, human nature can work against us." He started to line up his shot, then turned back to me and said, "When I took lessons from the golf pro, he gave me drills to practise. At the next session, he could tell right away whether I had followed his advice. Following the process he had outlined helped me to improve my game. When advisors lack process, it's harder for them to advise clients, because their execution is completely random. When all parties agree to a written plan, it's easier for everyone to adhere to it." He hit his final shot onto the last green.

"Nice shot!" I said. "The lessons seem to have paid off. One more question. Assuming the boomers follow your strategy, how do they become financially successful?" I asked.

"Oh, is that all you want to know?" We both started to laugh.

I shot 52 on the back nine for a perfect 104. Not a bad round, but there's still room for improvement if I want to be able to hit 100 by the time I'm a centenarian. Andrew shot an impressive 83, something I'll just have to dream about. We headed over to the deck for a quick drink.

"Okay, here's the boomers' solution in a nutshell. We tell all our clients this recipe. Some are more successful at following it than others," Andrew said.

"I'm all ears," I responded.

"First, they have to put together a life plan. Write down all the things they want to accomplish, and prioritize them. Discuss them with spouses and family members who will be affected, and who will aid in the plan. Develop what Tony Robbins has called 'a compelling future.' We can point clients in a certain direction, but this plan is really up to them. Second, and this is where we get involved, they have to create a financial plan, a written document that prioritizes funds and cash flows towards the realization of their goals. The key is that both the life plan and the financial plan are written and in perfect sync with each other. And finally there is the execution, a written investment policy statement that guides them through the markets so they can execute their plan. This document needs to describe risk tolerance, asset mix and all parties' roles and expectations."

"Sounds pretty impressive."

"Basic stuff. You want to build a house, you need a plan. You want a great life, you need a plan. You want your assets to do well—"

"You need a plan." We laughed.

"If everyone followed a process like that, the markets would be very stable in the future. Investors would thrive, advisors would be happier, and the average person would do better. But you have to keep on top of your plan. You must continually review all aspects of it, and all parties need to communicate with each other."

I was exhilarated. It is always a delight to speak to someone who thinks a great deal about his chosen vocation. But I was also feeling a little sheepish for having picked Andrew's brain for the past four hours.

"Buying you a pop doesn't seem a fair bargain, somehow, for the amount of information you've shared with me today." I grinned.

"Oh, I wouldn't worry. I have plans for how you can repay me," Andrew said, returning the grin.

He had my attention now. "What did you have in mind?"

"Jamie mentioned that you and your wife are writing a book. If I understand the nature of the book, it would be perfect for my clients. I'd like to give you my thoughts on how consumers could improve their outcomes in the capital markets. Would you be open to including some of these ideas in your book?"

"I'm not just open to it—I think it's a terrific offer!" Andrew's input would add to the book's value immeasurably. This wasn't theory, it was research from someone on the front lines with significant experience.

"Well, Jamie and I would both be happy to help in any way we can. It will benefit us, too, by giving us a tool to help our clients."

We agreed to meet again the following week in Andrew's office. Golfing is great, but sitting at a conference table will allow us to focus more on the discussion. The next topic: real estate, and how it relates—or rather correlates—to the markets and asset mix.

To say I could hardly wait would be putting it mildly.

7
Reporting to Yourself

MEREDITH

Since our meeting with Jamie, my mind has been racing. Perhaps the best thing our advisors can do for us is to get us to focus on what the issues are in our lives. To act as guides, because in the end, imposed solutions aren't going to work. We need to struggle and reason and consider the problems ourselves; inevitably, we will come up with a workable solution.

On the golf course, Jamie asked Pieter to consider what he was doing in the market. The answer wasn't easy, but the very act of thinking about it started us on the path to a solution to our struggles with our investments. In his office, Jamie asked us a similar and significantly more important question: What are you trying to do with your lives? As he pointed out, we invest simply to finance the life we want to live. To achieve our goals, it is imperative that we know how we want life to unfold. As Stephen Covey says, "Start with the end in mind." I had put *The Seven Habits of Highly Effective People* on my shortlist of things to read.

The biggest issue Jamie raised with Pieter and me was accountability. He asked us to think about how companies operate: not only do they plan, but people at all levels have someone they report to. He suggested it should work that way with our finances. A good plan will allow us to track how we're doing relative to our goals, and will make us accountable. The advisor is accountable to the client and vice versa. He stressed that it is also important that we are accountable to ourselves.

From a sociological point of view, the boomers' struggle to fund retirement is intriguing. Why are so many of us having such a difficult time? At a time of such considerable wealth, why are there so many people who cannot seem to take control of their financial lives? Part of the solution has to be that they cannot take control of their lives as a whole, let alone the financial aspects.

Life has changed for Canadians. We are now living more harried lives. As Faith Popcorn suggested in her famous *Popcorn Report*, we're trying to live "99 lives," and many of us are failing miserably. We need to remind ourselves that the capitalist system was designed to produce and distribute the highest level of goods and services, not to deliver the highest level of peace and happiness. We have to create those for ourselves.

After our meeting with Jamie, I'd wanted to wait a few days before beginning the first phase of our life plan: dreaming and goal setting. I suggested to Pieter that over the next few days we should each start to write down some ideas about what our future should look like. Being the practical one, I gave him some questions to consider, so we would be on the same page when our discussion started in earnest. I kept it simple, listing the following:

1. When do we want to retire?
2. Are we looking for full or partial retirement?

3. What activities do we want to pursue in retirement, and what travel plans do we want to make?
4. What are our goals before retirement?
5. How can we plan for any health issues that might arise?
6. What is our plan for our estate?

As Jamie advised us, goals and objectives will change and adjust; what's important is to start the process. We decided to begin our discussion on Tuesday, when Emily was leaving for a friend's cottage for a few days. Pieter had volunteered to drive her to the cottage, forty minutes north, in the Gatineau hills.

"How was the Feldmans' cottage?" I asked, when Pieter returned after dropping Emily off.

"Beautiful. It's a gorgeous piece of property. I can hardly wait to go up to our place next week," Pieter replied.

We hadn't yet been up to our cottage this year because we'd been so busy. But then, who am I kidding? We're always busy. I was anxious for some time away from the hustle and bustle of everyday life, and, yes, away from thoughts of life plans and finances. But for now we had to get those issues out of the way so we'd be able to truly relax during our two weeks at the cottage.

We fixed a couple of sandwiches and got down to work.

"I guess the first thing to think about," I began, "is why we were unable to follow through on the plan we made several years ago. When Hazen first got us interested in our finances, we went through all the right steps, I thought. And yet we weren't able to keep our investments on track."

"That's exactly what's been bothering me. What went wrong?"

"Well, actually, a lot went right," I responded. "We set up college plans for the kids; we started to think about our finances and our investments; and we started to pay close attention to the markets."

"Maybe too close," Pieter suggested.

"Perhaps. But we made a pretty good stab at it, and now we don't have to start from scratch. I think Jamie has a point: doing the right things isn't enough; we have to tie everything in to a plan."

"It reminds me of the old story about taking a fool and motivating him to work. In the end, all you've got is a motivated fool. Maybe I'm being too tough on myself, but I feel like that fool. I was motivated to finance our future, but I really didn't know what I was doing."

I suddenly felt awkward. I wanted Pieter to focus on the positive. We had gone through a rough period lately, and we had been through several in the past. But I wanted to use our troubles as a learning experience, and I sensed serious planning was the key to success.

"I've thought a lot about what Jamie said the other day," I said. "One of his key messages is that the proper plan allows you to focus. Let's face it, Pieter, we were subjected to a lot of conflicting messages. Hype about the markets, friends adding advice, the incessant drone of the media—it's no wonder many Canadians have a hard time focusing on the task at hand. Jamie is right that investing has to have a purpose that all parties agree to, and that the plan must be written down. Take a look at this." I handed an article to Pieter. It was a study done by Yale University with the graduating class of 1953. The researchers asked the new grads if they had written down a summary of goals and objectives for their lives. These could be financial goals or personal or career-related goals. Only 3 percent of the grads had a written plan. Twenty years later, the researchers revisited the grads to see how they were doing. The 3 percent who'd had a plan were outperforming the others in every aspect of their lives, and especially financially. In fact, the combined net worth of that 3 percent was greater than the combined net worth of the remaining 97 percent. Obviously, having a plan can't hurt.

Pieter had a quick look through the article and looked up at me. "It's powerful stuff, I agree, but here's my problem: I feel it's all a little too simplistic. We follow a magical path from a life plan to a financial plan to an investment plan, and *voilà*, we hit retirement nirvana. We tell Jamie the details, and he plugs them into a mathematical model, and all our problems are solved. I do like the notion of a plan, but rates of return and market performance have to come into play somewhere. There's no use building a well-designed bridge if the lumber's no good."

Trust Pieter to come up with an engineering analogy. But he had hit on one of my greatest concerns. The large swings in the value of our accounts had caused me a great deal of grief. I'd resigned myself to the fact that I was not a very good investor. "I hear what you're saying, honey," I said, "but what have we got to lose? We're certainly not doing very well without a plan. I think we should take this opportunity to create a better course of action, one we can have confidence in and stick with. So why don't we give it a chance?"

Pieter nodded and handed me the financial workbook Jamie had given us. True to his nature, Pieter had spent a couple of nights working through it. I'm not sure if it's his engineering background or his parents' influence, but my husband is a bit of a stickler about keeping records. Our lack of success in the markets certainly wasn't due to lack of organization or effort.

I flipped the booklet open and reviewed our financial data. The first page was standard stuff, a list of all our personal information. It also had a place for the names and numbers of advisors such as our lawyer, accountant, banker, insurance agent, and so forth. This tacit suggestion that all these folks should be working together on our behalf was interesting. I made a note to talk to Jamie about it. Our bank accounts, safety deposit box numbers, wills and powers of attorney were also listed.

Our assets and liabilities filled up the next two pages. Computer programs make the tracking of assets a whole lot easier, as Pieter had learned while putting this information together. A cash-flow analysis followed, and I paused for a moment to look it over. Because Pieter kept accurate records of all our bank statements and credit card bills, the analysis gave a very clear picture of how we were spending our money.

Two thoughts ran through my mind as I reviewed the columns for the past year. The first was that we didn't really have a budget. We talk about money a great deal, and I think we have a sense of priorities, but we don't have formal discussions about finances. The second was something Jamie had mentioned at our meeting that had really stuck with me. He said that most Canadians don't have a revenue problem, they have a spending problem. In other words, their revenues don't match their expenditures. His conclusion was that people lack a plan that will ensure their income and expenses match within a reasonable margin of error. Looking closely, most of our expenses made sense, but there were certainly some we could have thought through more. Just going through this part of the exercise struck me as useful.

As I got to the final pages, I came upon a section titled Personal and Financial Goals. Pieter had scribbled in goals in a few places, but then had crossed them out. He had pretty much left the pages blank.

"Why is this part not filled out?" I asked.

"I found filling it out as challenging as answering the question of what we are doing in the markets." Pieter responded. "And I realized I couldn't fill it out without your input. Look at the first question: What is your most urgent financial concern? We should be able to answer that in a second, but somehow I don't think we've discussed it enough. And a computer is not going to be a help with this stuff."

"Well, Jamie warned us that this part would go slowly. But we've got to figure it out. It's going to be more and more important to have a plan as we get older. Why don't we start by going through those questions I came up with last week?"

I took out my list. "So, when do we want to retire?"

Pieter looked at me as if to say, "You know the answer to this one," and smiled. "Never," he replied.

We had discussed this before. Pieter has always felt that retiring means you are getting ready to die. Instead of flat-out retiring, he wants to remain involved in a company or in several ventures on a reduced basis. Recent data from

Statistics Canada seem to support his notion of retirement. A clear majority of Canadians approaching the traditional retirement age have indicated a desire to continue to be active in the economy. They want to work!

I, too, feel I will want to keep working well past the age of sixty-five. But who knows how I'll feel when it actually arrives? It's still a ways off! "I can't imagine myself just sitting around," I said. "Look at Hazen and Ruth—they're both still going strong."

"Well," Pieter replied, "there's no reason you should have to. You're self-employed—no one is going to be edging you out of the workforce as you get older."

"That's true. I can take work on or not, depending on how I feel about it when the time comes. It would be nice if our finances were in good enough shape that we didn't need my income, though. I can see myself doing a bit of volunteer work." I knew from my studies of aging populations that older people tend to be among the most active volunteers, and I certainly liked the idea of working to help others. "Working with the elderly would be a natural for me, since I missed that time with my parents. I still can't quite accept the fact that they died so young."

"I know what you mean. And I think that's a terrific idea. Okay, so that's something to put into our life plan: we'd like to have enough money to live off comfortably if you aren't bringing in an income," Pieter said.

"Well, really, it would be great if neither of us had to bring in any money. I know, I know—you're not going to retire at sixty-five. But, Pieter, not working doesn't have to mean you're not useful. If we're secure in our finances by the time we hit sixty-five, anything more we bring in will be gravy. I think we should plan for that. That way, if, heaven forbid, one of us should get sick..."

"I don't even want to think about that. Let's look at it from a more positive angle instead. If we're financially stable, we'll be able to take time off to travel. Remember how great it was in Rome? We always meant to go back."

Pieter and I had travelled before we were married and had planned to keep travelling. But the arrival of our children had changed all that. We kept thinking we would have time to travel "next year." But next year never seemed to come, as the reality of life with babies, then school kids, then teenagers took its toll on our lives as individuals and as a couple. Don't get me wrong—the experience of being a mother isn't something I would ever trade. Malcolm and Emily have fulfilled me in a way nothing else possibly could have, and I cannot imagine life without them. But travel plans had fallen by the wayside. Now one of our children was in university, and the second wasn't far off. It was both daunting and exciting: we were about to get our freedom back. "Let's not wait until we're retired to start travelling again," I said. "Once Emily is off to university, we'll have more time for ourselves. Do you think we could work a yearly trip into our life plan?"

"I'd like that," Pieter said. We agreed that early each year we would figure out our travel plans for the year ahead. We also established a list of places we would like to visit. Italy topped the list; although we had been there before, it seemed as if Pieter's Italian heritage was drawing him back, and I couldn't argue with that! But I was also eager to see parts of the world I hadn't seen before: the rest of Europe,

Japan, Brazil, Australia, the pyramids in Egypt. Really, I wanted to see as many different places and experience as many different cultures as I could. The one thing neither of us had any interest in was going on a cruise. As Emily would say, "That's for old people!" But my real issue with cruises is they just don't give you enough time to immerse yourself in the culture of the places you visit.

An annual vacation would certainly take planning, both from a logistical and a financial standpoint. We hoped that the financial plan that stemmed from our life plan could make it work for us. After all, that's what a financial plan is for: to help us achieve our dreams. And travelling was a big dream, for both of us. Luckily, we can do without luxury accommodations. As long as the rooms are clean and bug-free, that's good enough for us!

Once we had some travel goals figured out, we moved on to other activities we might want to pursue in our retirement. It seemed funny to be thinking about what I might want to do with my time twenty-odd years from now, but anything that doesn't bring in money takes it away, so our plan needed to take these activities into account. Pieter, of course, wanted to work on his golf game, and he suggested that I start playing with him. He told me he sees a lot of retired couples hanging out together on the course. He tried to convince me it would be good exercise, but I was on to him: it would be good for his manly ego to feel he can teach me a thing or two. But there has to be give and take in our relationship.

"Okay, here's the deal," I said. "I'll take up golf, but you have to come to yoga with me. Oh—and I'm considering taking up pottery."

I wasn't serious about the pottery; I just wanted to see Pieter's reaction. And the look on his face before I let him off the hook was priceless.

The next item on my list was goals before retirement. "The big one, of course," I said, "is to get the mortgage paid off." We were currently amortizing the mortgage over twenty years, but had been hoping to speed that up. Now that I was going back to work, we could focus a good part of my income on this goal. We mentioned this to Jamie, and he said he would draw up a schedule that would allow us to retire the mortgage before we hit sixty.

Pieter and I had different career goals. His company was doing very well, and he was looking to expand, perhaps take over or merge with another company. He will always find a way to work; he'd drive us both crazy otherwise. As far as my career was concerned, I wanted some intellectual challenge. It wasn't about the money—I just wanted to explore what I could do. I knew I wasn't alone in this: there are an enormous number of well-educated women looking to re-enter the workforce. Ruth has told me she is fascinated by this trend and can't wait to see how it plays out.

Next, despite Pieter's reluctance, we really did have to talk about our health. It was a difficult topic for us. My parents had both died in their early sixties; they didn't make it to retirement. Pieter's dad had passed away a few years ago, but his mother was still going strong. Pieter and I were fully aware of the health problems that face older Canadians, and we knew what we needed to do: stay fit. A recent cover article in *Time* magazine discussed the issues of health and aging in depth. There seem to be some common traits in healthy older people: they are positive, they stay active, and they generally eat well. As the article pointed out, there are no overweight centenarians.

I wondered whether many Canadians factor health maintenance into their future plans. Awareness about health has certainly increased, but despite that, obesity rates are on the rise, along with the myriad of health problems associated with extra weight. Yet there seems to be a gym on every corner. Of course, there is usually a fast-food joint right next door.

The next item on my list was estate planning, but we decided to table that for the time being. We felt we needed professional advice on that topic.

We were left with a list of our future goals and dreams. And that's what we did for the rest of the night: we dreamed. We talked for hours, and it was wonderful. We have many dreams in common, as well as some that are clearly individual—and that's okay.

This chat was long overdue. When we were first married, we used to talk about our dreams all the time. A lot of these talks, of course, centred around what our children would look like and what we would name them. But we also dreamed about buying the perfect house and how we would furnish it. We dreamed about how our careers would take shape. Now I realized how apt Ruth's idea of halftime is. Pieter and I really are at halftime: our children are almost grown, we're gradually paying off the mortgage on our house, and our careers are in full swing. We've fulfilled our early dreams, and it's time to create some new ones.

When I shared these thoughts with Pieter, he ran with the sports analogy, pointing out that the great coaches are those who can adjust their game plans at halftime. Likewise, we need to continually review our game plan. It must be flexible so we can modify it as our lives change and we see what life sends our way.

By bedtime we felt we had made a great start. We had some concrete issues we wanted to deal with immediately: paying off a debt we had taken on for a bathroom renovation and detailing a plan for retiring our mortgage. Other areas were clearly a work-in-progress—it would take time before we were clear on how they fit in to the overall plan. We decided to ask Jamie to help us prioritize our financial goals at our next meeting.

The process was invigorating, but it wasn't often that we had the house to ourselves. Leaving our developing life plan behind for the night, we headed up to bed.

8
Slow Down—You're Moving Too Fast

MEREDITH

"Whew! I didn't think I'd make it in time," I said to Ruth. "What a rush Saturday mornings are at our house."

I met her in the parking lot of Pratt's Garden Centre. I'd called her during the week to arrange another meeting to continue our discussions of the "state of the world as we know it." I'd lent her a book, *The Paradox of Choice* by Barry Schwartz, and wanted to hear her take on it. She agreed to meet, but on one condition: we had to meet on Saturday morning at the garden centre of her choice. What, I'd asked, is this all about? She assured me she'd make everything clear when we met at Pratt's. So here I was—in a parking lot.

It had been our usual crazy Saturday morning hustle. Emily has turned into quite the avid soccer player, and her coach has scheduled 7:30 practices for every Saturday during the summer. It always seems tougher to get up early on a Saturday than on any other day. Pieter and I usually had a little tiff on Friday evening over who would get the chore of driving Emily across town for the practice. If I was going to be a soccer mom, he was going to take his rightful place as a soccer dad.

This Saturday morning, Pieter got to sleep in. I'd sped across town from the soccer field to meet Ruth for 8:00 sharp. Sure enough, there she was in the parking lot—car door open—pouring coffee from her Thermos.

"I hope you have some there for me too," I said, after giving her a quick hug.

"Sure do. I decided to bring my own coffee this morning, rather than stop at a coffee shop. I just wasn't in the mood for all the choices they give you: tall, grande, venti—what next?" she replied, handing me a steaming cup.

I took a sip. "So, why are we here?" I asked, gesturing around the grounds of the garden centre. Pratt's is a huge place, reputedly the best in the city.

"Because it proves a point. I am in complete agreement with the book you lent me. There's way too much choice in this world. And even though Pratt's is one of my favourite places, it puts the burden of choice squarely on the consumer's shoulder. Quite frankly, Pratt's complicates my life needlessly."

"What the heck are you talking about?" I laughed. This is just like Ruth, I thought. She's dragged me out here to prove her point and give me a lecture to boot. Always the teacher...

"Finish your coffee first, then I'll show you," she answered. "I want to talk to you about too many choices and too little time in all our lives, but particularly in the lives of the baby boomers. Here you are, squealing in on a perfect summer Saturday morning, and the first thing out of your mouth is what a rush you're in. And it's only 8:00 A.M.!"

"Welcome to my world. I'm in a constant hurry, what with Emily and her activities, Pieter and his work, helping you and Hazen plan your book, the driving, the groceries, keeping up the house—and sometimes, believe it or not, I like to squeeze in a minute or two of downtime, just to catch my breath."

"What's all this rushing about? Why do boomers worship at the alter of Busyness?"

Leave it to Ruth to already have her finger on something I'd been pondering. Since Pieter and I had our planning discussion a few days ago, I've been wondering about my penchant for running from pillar to post at the fastest speed possible. How could I get our household to slow down a bit?

Funny, I'd always thought of my busyness as an accepted element of being part of the baby boom generation. When I look back at my childhood, it seems my parents simply had less to do than we do today. Although when I brought the topic up recently with my favourite aunt, she threw it back into my lap. "Excuse me, sweetheart," she'd responded calmly. "Let me remind you that I had five kids, a wringer washer and a clothesline. I had plenty to keep me busy. Seems to me that a lot of your running is self-imposed. Think of all the driving you've done over the years, taking your kids to piano, skiing, soccer, karate, swimming. Those lessons have exposed Malcolm and Emily to wonderful things. But have they all really been necessary?" I was angry with her at the time. Certain family members do seem to be able to push your buttons. My kids wanted to do those things; I wasn't forcing activity upon them. And why would I deprive them of the chance to be well rounded? But thinking about that conversation now—after reading *The Paradox of Choice* and talking with Jamie—I could appreciate her comments in a different light. She wasn't putting me down, she was simply questioning my choices. Did I have to be the one to drive them everywhere? Weren't there other options? That was the issue in a nutshell—not enough planning. It always seems to boil down to the "p" word: planning.

"You're right. Speed has become a sort of religion for the boomers," I answered, sipping my coffee slowly, hoping to impress Ruth with my ability to relax and savour a good cup of java. "I think, in part, it's a desire to compete. If you're rushing around, it shows that you're in the game. If you're busy, you're successful. If you're relaxed, you're a loser."

I told Ruth about Pieter's friend Tom. Tom, Pieter and a couple of other guys have taken a two-day ski holiday every February for the past ten years. In the beginning, Tom, a corporate lawyer, always brought along a fax machine. Now he's replaced the fax machine with a cellphone, a printer and a BlackBerry. At lunch he heads back to the chalet to catch a few minutes of work. The other guys always figured this was Tom's way of showing them how indispensable—and thus important—he was. But, as Pieter pointed out, no truly urgent work ever seems to come Tom's way during their time at the ski hill.

"That compulsion or desire—whatever it is—to keep working 'round the clock' does take a toll, you know," Ruth said, nodding as I told my tale of Tom. "How's Tom's marriage, by the way? And his relationship with his kids?"

"Interesting you should ask. His marriage is lousy, and he doesn't spend any time at all with his kids."

"Tom is just one story, but research shows that this rush-rush-rush mentality is taking its toll in increased numbers of stress-related illnesses, absences from work and people simply burning out at a very young age. Did you know, for example, that we now sleep ninety minutes less a night than people did a century ago? And we need sleep—it's the great restorative that keeps us going."

"Okay, I don't need to be convinced. I just need to know how to get off the treadmill." I handed my empty cup back to Ruth.

"Well, let's take a leisurely stroll through the gardens and chat about that," Ruth said, taking my arm and leading me into a field of perennials. "Look around. What do you see?"

"I see thousands and thousands of hostas."

"Precisely." She laughed. "Ralph Waldo Emerson once said, 'The field cannot be well seen from within the field.' You're in the middle of a huge generation, all of whom are marching along, graduating from school, then establishing themselves in the work world and having children, investing, buying, consuming—and not really thinking too much about whether this is exactly what they want to do. When you're in the middle of everything, as Emerson says, it's tough to get to a high enough vantage point to see things as they really are. You only see lots of hostas."

We both laughed. "Lots of hostas to choose from," I replied. "Maybe this is a good time to talk about *The Paradox of Choice*. The author talks a lot about the time crunch. And one of the critical reasons we now feel so busy is that so much of our lives is devoted to making choices—among food products, places to vacation, activities for our kids, brands of running shoes—you name it, there's so much of it out there. When I was a kid and went with my mother to buy plants, there were only two choices. Pink petunias or white petunias. Life was simpler then."

"And what does Schwartz suggest as one of the ways to wade through today's deluge of choices?"

"I know, I know. Planning: formulating some rules and standards to live by. Then sticking to them. Pieter and I spent some serious time last week talking about planning— both our lives and our finances. It's not that easy, you know."

"Of course, I know that." Ruth smiled and handed me a hosta with a tag that told me it was a slug-resistant variety called 'Great Expectations.' "This will be a perfect colour beside my new clematis. Raising Dylan and working my way through the university world of tenure and publications, I had to have a plan to achieve everything I wanted to—without driving myself around the bend. As Schwartz advises in his book, you can't begin to start choosing wisely until you have developed a clear understanding of your goals. You have to recognize that with choice comes stress. The trick is to navigate yourself through the maze of choices. I see it as an efficient trip to the grocery store: have a plan, stick to it and learn from your choices, but don't revisit them. In other words, formulate a good general life plan—think ahead to what you want to achieve, and trust yourself and those around you. Then go for it and don't spend much time looking back."

"So, where did you start?"

"Schwartz says the first choice is the critical one, and that's between the goal of having everything in your life 'just right' and the goal of having things that are 'good enough.' Remember, I didn't have the advantage of reading

The Paradox of Choice. I was making these decisions thirty years ago, long before the book was published. And it was a very easy choice for me—I opted for 'good enough.' I knew that to accomplish everything I wanted to, I could not physically afford to check out and examine all the possible choices available to me. I would have gone without sleep for thirty years. I was too busy housecleaning, gardening, writing books and papers, and bringing up Dylan—with Hazen's help, of course. So I made the decision to forge ahead, not to look back with regret, but to get on with my life. There were lots of choices I just never bothered to consider. I had my goals clearly in mind, and I stuck to them. We had dust bunnies under our beds, Dylan never took tae kwon do lessons, we ate frozen lasagne lots of nights. I made compromises, but I also got a lot accomplished—and I kept my sanity and my sense of humour. Dylan turned out okay too."

"You're what Schwartz calls a 'satisficer'—you've got your standards, but you know when to settle for something that's good enough. Unlike a 'maximizer,' you don't need perfection," I said.

"Yup—that's me—a satisficer. And, if I'm not mistaken, you're on your way to becoming one too."

"I know I am. I have to admit that I do have a tendency to weigh all the choices available, but I'm trying to put that behind me as I work towards developing a life plan. I've stripped down my goals. I know that I want to give both Malcolm and Emily the option of attending university. Malcolm's already there, and I hope that Emily will want to go when the time comes. Pieter and I will support them during their university years, but we also expect both to contribute, by working summer jobs, for example. I also know that I want to work for myself. I want the emotional space in my life that being self-employed provides. I know self-employment is challenging and often unpredictable. But I'm ready for that—it's one of my most important goals, and it's fundamental to my life plan. I also want to prepare for retirement, both financially and emotionally. But I don't really feel the need—at least not now—to retire at sixty-five. I like to work. I see myself working in some way, maybe part-time, maybe volunteering, until I'm in my early seventies. I know Pieter feels the same way."

"You're on your way, Meredith," Ruth replied, handing me another hosta, this one a sun-tolerant variety called 'Abba Dabba Do.' "And you're doing it the way author Stephen Covey recommended in *The Seven Habits of Highly Effective People*: 'Start with the end in mind.' Enough talk for the moment. I have to get serious here and choose some good-enough plants for my gorgeous garden."

As Ruth started off down the garden path, I marvelled at the coincidence: both Ruth and Jamie had quoted Stephen Covey. I really must start thinking about "the end."

We spent the next hour working our way through the fields and greenhouses of Pratt's. I was responsible for lugging the wagon that Ruth filled with her choices. She was—as she said—practical in the way she made her selections. A true satisficer. She had a list of plants she wanted and a budget, and she didn't stray from either. That meant we moved through Pratt's very efficiently. Instead of spending the day muddling through the thousands of choices, we were standing at the cash, ringing up her purchases, before ten.

"Great," Ruth said, tucking her wallet back into her purse. "I've got all day to get these plants into the garden. I have a big favour to ask of you. Will you come home with me and help me unload this jungle?" She gestured to the mass of plants on the wagon.

"No problem. Let's get cracking."

I followed Ruth home in my car. She led the way, speeding as usual. We often laughed about her penchant for fast driving. So measured in all other aspects of her life, Ruth has a "need for speed"—just one of the personality quirks that make her unpredictable and interesting. It is always a challenge to keep up with her.

Even though my driving on the way home was quicker than usual, the time alone gave my mind some space to wander and a chance to develop a clearer view of our morning discussion. The boomers' march through the North American economy had created a culture of consumerism during the 1980s and 1990s, and it wasn't showing signs of slowing in the 2000s. We have friends who are constantly upgrading their homes, buying cottages that are more like upscale condos and taking fabulous trips to villas in Umbria, ski holidays in St. Moritz and cruises to the Greek islands. I hear the voice of my mother echoing in my ears when I look at these friends. She always felt that people were too caught up in buying things just for the sake of owning more stuff. She'd quote Ann Landers: "You can't have everything. Where would you put it?" I laughed as a kid. As an adult, I understand, and now the comment seems more troubling than funny.

I have to keep reminding myself that these wealthy boomers are the few, and that many boomers are much more like Pieter and me: working hard to make ends meet. But, as Jamie says, maybe we have a spending problem, not a revenue problem. We boomers have always competed with one another—for spaces in graduate school, in jobs, in homes. And now our children are competing in the same way. It's interesting how we, as parents, respond to this competitive environment. Boomers—Pieter and I are no different—want our children to have the best.

I realize now that the desire for the best is one of the key underpinnings of the time crunch in which I find myself so often embroiled. Last spring a friend lent me a book by Anna Quindlen, a columnist for *Newsweek*. In *Loud and Clear*, Quindlen expounds on how boomer parents have created the time monster. According to Quindlen, North American kids have lost about four unstructured hours a week in the last twenty years. We now have perpetually busy, overscheduled children. We've moulded them in our own hyper-busy image. And yet, as Quindlen details in her book, there is ample psychological research to suggest that what we might call "doing nothing" is when human beings actually do their best thinking, and when creativity comes to call.

All the hustle is about competing—and winning. God forbid a boomer should be a loser.

I followed Ruth onto her street. As I parked, I concluded my inner rant, wondering whether the need to win and the need to show those around you that you *can* win is simply basic human nature, nothing more than a combination of greed and jealousy. We boomers are no different from the generations that preceded us and those that will follow us. There just happen to be a lot of us.

"Let me give you two a hand," Hazen said, emerging from the house as Ruth and I pulled up to the curb.

"Thanks, Hazen. We're taking everything right around to the backyard," Ruth said.

"This is great timing—both of you here together," Hazen said. "I've been jotting some ideas down for our book. Anyone interested in hearing them?"

"Oh—I get the drift," Ruth replied smartly. "You're going to stand in the backyard and hold forth, while Meredith and I do the dirty work."

"Precisely." Hazen chuckled. "I don't want to interfere with your aesthetic vision for the garden. You know where things should go, not me."

"Well, he's good for entertainment value, Ruth," I said. "Sort of like listening to the radio."

"Okay—we're on for the lecture, Hazen. But not until you've done your job of carrying plants to the back," Ruth said.

After a few trips back and forth to the car, we'd brought everything to the garden. Hazen came out the back door of the house with a red file folder and a couple of books in hand.

"I want to talk about three ideas I feel we should include in our book: status anxiety, slowing down and trustmarks," Hazen said, lowering himself into a Muskoka chair near the fountain.

"I understand the slowing down part," I said. "In fact, Ruth and I spent a fair bit of this morning talking about my need to pull the plug on speed. But what do you mean by status anxiety and trustmarks?"

"*Status Anxiety* is a new book by Alain de Botton. It

analyzes our anxiety about what others think of us," Hazen replied.

"Like in high school when you thought everyone was looking at you?" I asked.

"Actually, you're not far off. It's the mature version of that anxiety, and boomers are truly plagued by it."

"You're telling me. Just drive around this neighbour-hood if you're in the mood to be judged. You're a winner if you have a Land Rover, a loser if you own a Hyundai. What's new about that?"

"Quite right. It's old news—the green-eyed monster has always been with us, together with the anxiety it generates. It's been exacerbated in the boomer world of SUVs, home theatres and Prada purses. I want to offer boomers a solution to that anxiety that frees them from it."

"What do you propose?" I asked.

"Something along the lines of what de Botton suggests. Boomers need to think bigger than they have been. They need to challenge the conventional wisdom and go beyond the constraints of society. And one of the ways they can do that is via the second idea I want to talk about today: slowing down. Did you know that one of the reasons baseball is losing its popularity in modern society is its slowness? It originally captured the imagination as a thinking person's game, full of strategy and thought, but it simply isn't fast enough to engage people who now live in a crazy, fast-forward world. Baseball is a game from a slower era. Today, people want basketball or hockey, where the action is non-stop. And yet it's only when we slow down that we are able to appreciate what's going on around us, spend quality time with our friends and family— take pleasure from what life has to offer."

Ruth piped up from the back of the garden, where she was planting a hosta. "It's easy to tell people this, but hard to actually achieve a slower pace. We have to give people a framework that shows them how to get off the fast track."

"That's the second book I've brought out with me," Hazen said. "It's called *In Praise of Slow*, by Carl Honoré. This fellow decided that slower is better, and then made it happen in his own life. You know, it all goes back to planning. If you create a life plan that sets limits and standards, you can easily achieve a slower pace."

"Give me an example," I demanded. I still thought it was easy to talk about slowing down, much harder to actually do it.

"I'll give you a couple. Make the decision to go out only one night of the weekend. Even if you and Pieter get more than one invitation, limit yourselves to one night out. Then spend a night at home enjoying each other, cooking a nice dinner and relaxing with a good bottle of wine. Just the two of you. Or, how's this? Make Sunday evening supper a tradition, the night you and Pieter make a home-cooked meal for yourselves and whichever children happen to be home. Have a sit-down dinner, spend the evening talking and, maybe, once the supper dishes are cleared away, play Monopoly or Scrabble. It's a few hours that you always have as family time. No TV, no activities. Slow, not fast."

"This all takes us right back to the need for a life plan," Ruth said. "These changes will not happen in our lives unless we spend some time thinking about them and figuring out how to accomplish them and, finally, commit to them."

"What was that other thing you were talking about, Hazen? Something about trust?" I asked.

"Right—trustmarks. It's a play on the term 'trademark,' and it's used in the cyberspace world to denote the Internet sites one can rely upon. In the book *Searching for Certainty*, authors Darrell Bricker and Edward Greenspon say that trustmarks go beyond a good name—they're all about trustworthiness. Without trust, economic relations sink, and the Internet goes with them. People must trust that businesses operating in cyberspace can deliver; otherwise, they won't deal with them. I think the idea has far broader application to the world of boomers. To make their lives fulfilling, people must learn to trust those around them, but not in a foolish, foolhardy 'trust everybody' sort of way."

"Meredith, I started the morning quoting Emerson, and I'm going to do it again," Ruth warned. "'Trust men and they will be true to you; treat them greatly and they will show themselves great.'"

"Well, that's definitely a change for you, Ruth," I replied. "You usually quote Uncle Jack. But I'd point out that, if we use that quote in the book, it should be updated to reflect our world—something like 'trust people,' not just men."

"Good point." Hazen laughed. "You're going to be very useful to us old fogeys. But the fundamental truth is the same. To achieve rich, pleasurable relationships with others, trust is essential. As the philosopher Kant tells us, if we never trusted anyone, we'd never learn anything useful from anyone. We'd never enter into a partnership or friendship, because the other person would be certain to let us down. Creating relationships built on trust starts at a very personal level. If we treat people with respect, tell them the truth and keep our promises, we will reap the benefits of relationships built on trust."

At that moment, the phone in my purse began ringing. It was Emily. Her practice had finished early, and she hoped I could come pick her up as soon as possible. She was still in job-search mode and wanted to spend as many Saturday hours as possible distributing résumés.

"Well, folks, nice talking to you about creating an ideal life, but now my real, rushed life has intruded," I said. "I've got to pick up Emily and, as usual, I'm in a hurry."

"Don't leave without this, then," Hazen said, handing me his copy of *In Praise of Slow*.

"I have to spend the rest of the weekend getting ready for our trip to the cottage. But once we're there, I'll definitely curl up with a cup of tea and read this—slowly. It's great research material," I said. I hustled out of the garden and back to my busy life.

9
Needs versus Wants

HAZEN

I was up early the morning I was to meet with Andrew at his office. I had a number of ideas racing through my head, and I was intrigued that I was headed into an investment firm to spend a good part of the morning talking about real estate. When I had a preliminary chat with Andrew a few days ago, he made it quite clear he was no expert on real estate. What he wanted to discuss was how it fit into the asset mix of the average Canadian. He had done a great deal of analysis on our emotional tie-in to real estate and how this affects our thinking. Real estate is king, he had stated, and it may tell us how we will affect other commodities as we age.

He had my interest, and I was keen to meet with him— and hopefully share some of the thoughts of an older observer. We had agreed to meet in his office at 9:30. I found this a little strange, since that's the exact time the investment markets open, but I was sure he would explain the timing to me when I arrived.

He greeted me in the reception area of his office and showed me into a small boardroom.

"Why don't we chat in here, where it's quiet and we won't be distracted?" he said, motioning me to follow him.

"I'm curious about how we are able to meet just as the markets are opening," I responded.

"What the markets do on a day-to-day or minute-to-minute basis has very little effect on one's ability to accumulate wealth." Andrew said. "If you want to trade, it makes sense to be glued to the screen. But we use the market as an asset class, a means to end, you might say. So I'm only interested in the long-term outlook. We need to have a long-term view of our assets, and that's why I'm so interested in looking at real estate as a commodity."

"So we need to think of real estate as an asset class and look at how it fits in with other investments we hold?"

"Exactly. There are four main asset classes in Canada—cash, real estate, stocks and bonds—and all of them are important, in that order. Cash flow is the single most important factor for any business or household, followed by shelter. The investments follow after the basic necessities are covered."

"And knowing how these asset classes fit together is critical for the average investor."

"It's all there is. That's what Jamie and I try to get our clients to focus on: asset mix. Have the right amount of assets in each area, rebalance those assets and think long term," Andrew said.

"Sounds easy enough," I replied with a smile.

"Easy," Andrew repeated, returning my smile. "I'm always reminded of the great Jim Rohn line from one of his motivational speeches: 'If it's easy to do, it's easy not to do.' On another matter, tell me how you're coming along with your book."

I had to stop and think for a minute. I hadn't expected to

talk about my project at this meeting. "We're still in the planning stages, but things are proceeding well. Our basic plan is to discuss the social and financial well-being of Canadians today."

"Well, anything I can do to help, don't hesitate to ask. As I've mentioned, your book will be an excellent tool for our clients."

He handed me several large folders, labelled Real Estate, Stocks, Bonds, Asset Mix, and Pension Issues. Each had a number of articles inside. "These are for you to take with you—I had my assistant make copies of some of my files."

"This is wonderful. I can see you're going to be a great help to us," I replied.

Andrew laughed. "I hope at least some of our ideas will be useful. Now let's get down to business and talk about real estate as an asset." He took out his file and flipped it open to some notes he had jotted down for our meeting. "The first point I want to make is that analysts across the board completely blew their predictions of the future value of real estate."

I couldn't help but break into a guilty smile. "I'm one of them."

"I know. I've read some of your articles. You'll find a piece in the folder that you wrote a decade ago suggesting that real estate was about to peak," Andrew replied.

"It just made sense, given the ages of the baby boomers. They had all the real estate they needed."

"That's the key word: 'need.' We misread our largest generation's understanding of 'needs' versus 'wants.' Now, don't feel bad, Hazen: I could show you ten books that showed a flat line for real estate. One analyst at Harvard predicted a 47 percent decline by the end of this decade."

"And they were all wrong," I said.

"Yes, and it's why they were wrong that's absolutely critical for us to grasp. We used the patterns of previous generations to predict what the baby boomers would do. Frankly, that was a mistake."

"If we've learned anything about this generation, it's that a great deal of them are free agents. They want to live life to the fullest."

"Well, just look at them. They are highly educated, and they grew up in an era of great economic and technological expansion and innovation. They're not going to settle; they're going to push the envelope, as they always have."

"They've certainly pushed the economy along as they've aged."

"That's another great point," Andrew said. "Real estate can only get this big if we have the economic wealth to back it up. The increased real estate valuations reflect how well we have done economically. We have the wealth, and we want to live better. It wasn't long ago that owning a home was a distant dream for the average Canadian. Now it's a basic expectation. Society changed, and along the way valuations changed to reflect the new realities."

"And *values* affected expectations as well. An American commentator once pointed out that the boomers' parents were brought up in the Depression. Their expectations weren't very high. Those same parents, almost as a reaction, raised their children to have high expectations. Times were good, and they've done well. On average, houses today are almost twice the size of the average home thirty years ago. We have things like family rooms and larger kitchens to reflect our changing values. And all this is because, by every economic measure, the boomers, in middle age, are the wealthiest generation in Canadian history—by a large margin," I said.

"That's true," Andrew said. "Inheritance has created wealth for this generation at a greater clip than ever before. We tend to inherit in our late forties, and the boomers are in their forties and fifties now. Because we are better educated today, we have a much higher per capita income than past generations did. Plus, families now tend to have two incomes. Boomers certainly have the money to spend. But I think there's another reason we underestimated real estate's ultimate value."

"And what's that?"

"It's not just that the boomers have the wealth to acquire large homes. They also have a need to put that wealth on display. You can hardly show your friends a copy of your investment statement. But you can demonstrate your success with a large house. Heck, your friends never even need to know how much of it you actually own. There has been a huge incidence of boomers in their early fifties buying the proverbial 'monster home.' And why did they do it?" Andrew asked.

"Because they can," I replied.

Andrew started to laugh. "You even have the boomer lingo down pat. After their kids moved out, they bought a huge house in a killer neighbourhood to satisfy their wants. Their parents would have focused on their *needs*, and that's where our predictions went wrong."

"So how does this relate to the investment markets?" I asked.

"Here's the question: If real estate changed as an asset, are other commodities going to be affected the same way in the future? Analysts have always assumed that assets have a constant valuation from generation to generation. This has certainly not been the case with real estate. Adjusting for inflation, homes are a greater asset in terms of real wealth for this generation than for any before them. Investment markets have also benefited, to a lesser degree, from this trend towards greater wealth, and I believe this will only get bigger over the next twenty years. You buy a home first, then you tend to work on your savings and investments as you get older."

Andrew took a breath while he let it all sink in and then continued. "Second, I would suggest that, in a passive way, most Canadians are quite competent at handling their real estate. On the other hand, unfortunately, many are actively incompetent at handling their investments. I'm always fascinated by the way investors react to different asset classes."

"Most Canadians don't see any long-term financial risk in owning a home," I replied.

"You're right. Most Canadians own one house and feel quite safe even if it's leveraged with a mortgage. But if it's so safe, why do they need to insure it to the rafters?" Andrew asked.

"I think I see where you're going with this," I said. "The risk on one home is absolute. That's why we need insurance. We could be wiped out by a fire or flood."

"That's right. If you owned a hundred houses, and they were geographically diversified, you wouldn't need insurance. At, let's say, $500 worth of insurance per house, you'd save $50,000 a year. After several years, if you had a problem with one of your houses, you could cover it your-self. Of course, people don't own a hundred houses, so the insurance companies act as intermediaries."

"So, stocks are like houses in that owning one is risky, but if you diversify and own a 'neighbourhood of stocks,' there is very little long-term risk. Investors simply react differently to these two capital assets."

"Exactly," Andrew said. "But even when they have diversified, many investors still aren't very good at managing their investments, and I believe it's because of the way they've been taught to think about the stock market. When they buy a home, most people think about the investment in twenty-year intervals. The stock market is often thought of in twenty-day intervals, or less. By focusing on the short term, we create great volatility in the market and, to some degree, become victims of our own habits."

"So, if investors could think longer term, they'd do much better?"

"It's fundamental. And if they could consider the risks of both assets, they'd be even better off. But because we know we are going to live in our homes for a long time, we don't worry much about the value or the risk. Other than rough estimates, we don't really know what it's worth, anyway. As a result, we convince ourselves that it's slowly moving up in value, and we relax for the ride."

"And that is clearly not how many investors react to the market," I said.

"Unfortunately not. The market is liquid, and it reports valuations every day, which is much of the problem. It's the old too-much-information syndrome again. There's an anec-dote I use to highlight the absurdity of the way we handle our investments. Jamie finds it quite amusing. The premise is that real estate, namely your house, trades on a market and you can get real-time quotes and potential buyers online."

"Interesting notion. That might create a little more volatility in the real estate market."

"It certainly would. The idea is that this guy has just accepted a bid online for his home, and it settles in one week. He calls home to speak with his wife. Their conversation goes like this:

HUSBAND: Hi, honey. Look, I was just online and I saw a great price for our house, so I took it.

WIFE: What do you mean you took it?

HUSBAND: I sold the house and got a great price.

WIFE: That's not funny. I know we talked about selling the house when the kids go off to school, but we can't sell yet.

HUSBAND: No, it's okay. I got a great price, and we can bid on a new place.

WIFE: You're not kidding... this is ridiculous—we're not moving.

HUSBAND: Closing is in one week. We can store our stuff until I close on a new place.

WIFE: But I love our house.

Andrew continued, "You can see where this is going. For obvious reasons, we don't speculate on our homes like that, so why would we speculate on other assets that way?"

"Well, if we did speculate on our homes, it would be great for movers and storage facility operators."

"Sure, and awful for realtors and home owners. I'm

certain speculators would quickly take advantage of the average person's skittishness with the market. Fortunately, the average person tends to buy and hold real estate, and as a result they make out okay."

"Oh, I think the average person does better than okay from their real estate. I've owned a home for many years and made quite a tidy profit from it," I replied.

"You're the exception to the rule, then. The average Canadian homeowner is unlikely ever to make a dime."

"That's a bold statement. I'd have to take exception to that claim."

"Just think about it," Andrew said. "Most Canadians reflect only on what they paid and what they sell for. There's a reason why the difference is tax-free: it's not really a gain at all. What they're missing are the taxes, the mortgage, the upkeep and, of course, because they're boomers, the renovations."

"So you believe these costs more than offset the gain?"

"For the average home owner, they do. Einstein said that compound interest is the eighth wonder of the world. The average Canadian has a mortgage on a considerable part of the home for more than twenty years. The interest adds up, unfortunately."

"You're not suggesting that owning a home is a bad idea, are you?" I asked.

"No, absolutely not. It's a great idea—as long as you know what a home really is: a terrific forced-savings vehicle. It's a great way to underpin financial stability, it's a superb part of our asset mix, and it's a great place to live."

"That's the whole point, isn't it? We need somewhere to live."

"Let me try out another scenario on you," Andrew said. "Imagine that you stay at a great hotel for the weekend. You have a great time, and as you're checking out, you compliment the manager and give him a bill for your stay."

"Seems a little ridiculous."

"If we eat out, we pay for dinner. And if we eat in, we pay for dinner. Either way, we need to eat. Whether we stay at a hotel or stay at home, we pay for our shelter. We have to live somewhere; it's simply a cost we bear. Many Canadians expect a positive return on their real estate. But over the long run, that's not likely to happen. I'm not dumping on real estate. It's a wonderful asset class, it correlates with other assets well, and it's nice to raise your children in a great neighbourhood. The point I'm trying to make is, consumers behave better with their real estate than with other assets such as the stock market. I've often told my clients that if they could treat all their assets as they treat real estate, they'd be a whole lot happier."

"I'm still not sure I agree with you on the returns for real estate."

"Let me show you some data," Andrew replied. He handed me a chart that showed the annual returns for real estate and the stock market for the past fifteen years.

As I was mulling over the chart, Andrew continued. "The data show a couple of clear outcomes. The average value for real estate in Ottawa went from $137,500 in 1990 to a recent value of $242,000. That's a return of roughly 76 percent over the fifteen-year period. That includes all residential housing, good and bad, for the period. During the same period, the TSE index appreciated 138 percent, from an index value of 3,561 to a recent close of 8,458. If we include dividends, the total return would be 222 percent. The returns on real estate and stocks are not even close."

	TORONTO STOCK EXCHANGE	OTTAWA REAL ESTATE
1990	−14.8%	2.9%
1991	12.0%	1.4%
1992	−1.4%	0.4%
1993	32.5%	3%
1994	−0.2%	−0.4%
1995	14.5%	−2.9%
1996	28.3%	−1.9%
1997	15.0%	2.4%
1998	−1.6%	0.1%
1999	31.7%	4.0%
2000	7.4%	6.6%
2001	−12.6%	10.3%
2002	−12.4%	14.1%
2003	26.7%	9.0%
2004*	1.1%	11.0%

* through June

"Interesting stuff," I replied.

"What's more interesting is how the appreciation in these two assets happened. Real estate was quite stable, while stocks were typically volatile—human nature and liquidity at work again! The investment markets consistently outperform the real estate market, yet investors are still convinced that a house is their best investment. Stocks create great anxiety because of their fluctuating values, and psychological studies have found that investors feel losses much more deeply than any pleasure they may feel from gains. That may explain their fondness for real estate."

"Couldn't someone argue that their real estate did much better than the average?" I tried playing devil's advocate.

"Sure, but you can make the same case for high-quality securities versus the index as a whole. Look, Hazen, I'm not making a case for securities over real estate. Actually, the two commodities work very well together. They tend to be countercyclical, which is great for investors: it's preferable to have complementary assets that move up and down at different times. Stocks had a great run in the nineties, when real estate was flat. Lately, real estate has exploded as the markets have stagnated. But what I'm trying to demonstrate is the paradoxical behaviour of the average investor. Investors often struggle in an asset class that has done quite well. I am absolutely convinced that volatility and the incessant reporting of valuations limit the potential outcomes for many investors."

"They need to have a plan, ignore the swings of the market as best they can and stick to the basics," I replied.

"Those are the keys. But, as an asset, real estate is much more easily understood and handled by investors," Andrew said.

"It's tangible, they look after it. Stocks tend to be more theoretical—they're pieces of paper for far-removed companies. Real estate and land, for that matter, are emotional. How many stories will we read today about people dying for companies? They do die for land. It's fundamental. I don't expect investors to connect with stocks and bonds as they do with their homes. I simply suggest they should consider why they've tended to deal well on an emotional level with their houses and see if they can apply those principles to other assets."

It appeared the sermon was done. I thanked Andrew for his thoughts and got up to leave. Andrew handed me a piece of paper. "I thought you could use this in your book somewhere. It's a quote I've always loved by a man named Jacob Fugger, who lived in the fifteenth century. His descendants in Europe are still wealthy to this day. 'Divide your fortune into four equal parts: stocks, real estate, bonds and gold coins. Be prepared to lose on one of them most of the time. During inflation, you will lose on bonds and win on gold and real estate; during deflation, you will lose on real estate and win on bonds, while your stocks will see you through both periods, though in a mixed fashion. Whenever performance differences cause a major imbalance, rebalance your fortunes back to the four equal parts.'"

"Sage advice."

"The only type of advice to listen to," Andrew said.

10
Future Funding Liabilities

PIETER

Meredith and I had spent two great uninterrupted weeks at our northern getaway on Wolf Lake. Emily came up with us and had some friends over off and on. It was a wonderful time to drink good wine, have great dinners and relax. I got through *The Da Vinci Code*, and Meredith got a head start on her book-club reading list for the fall. It was amazing how fast the time flew by, but we did get a chance to discuss some of our long-term dreams and aspirations. The timing for our next meeting with Jamie was perfect: it was set for Tuesday the week we got back.

When we arrived this time, he greeted us and showed us into his office. The meeting room we met in first, he explained, was where he met clients for informal chats. His office, which we were now entering, was where he got down to business. His assistant offered us coffee—exactly what I needed before taking on the task of planning the rest of my life. Jamie's office was quite small and had a number of charts on the walls. I wasn't quite sure what they were, but I had a sense we were about to find out.

"So, how was your break up north?" Jamie asked, as we settled into his office.

"Perfect," I responded. "It was just what we needed. And it was a great opportunity to talk over the issues you brought up at our last meeting."

Jamie took some papers out of a file and continued, "Always remember, your life is a work-in-progress. We tend to be successful when we talk over the challenges we face as they come up."

With that, Jamie handed a copy of a document to each of us. On the cover were our names and its title: Financial Plan and Investment Policy Statement.

"I received the financial planning workbook you folks completed, and I've put together this plan for you. Believe me, while you were relaxing at your cottage, I was here, working away! I want to go through this document with you so you get a general sense of where things are and what priorities we need to establish to get you to the preliminary goals you've outlined," Jamie explained.

"So, how do things look?" I asked, in that nervous way you ask your doctor how things are at the end of your annual physical.

"Actually, Pieter, you'll be happy to know that things don't look bad at all. Remember what I told you at our first meeting about the four pillars of wealth? Well, you're well on your way. You and Meredith are trying to live within your means, and are tracking expenses. The key will be to establish a more formal budget. You have some debt that I think you'd like to clean up, and you'll see in the plan that you should be able to retire all of your debt well before you hit sixty-five. You've also shown good discipline in saving and have established quite a nest egg in your RRSPs."

"That's the problem: how do we make sure we don't blow that nest egg on bad investment decisions?"

"The key to answering that question is in the fourth pillar—pension plans," Jamie responded.

Pension plans were what had discouraged us. If one of the characteristics of wealthy Canadians is that they are beneficiaries of good pension plans, we were out of luck—neither of us is ever going to be employed by a company that provides a pension plan. But as Jamie continued, my outlook changed.

"From here on in, I'd like your mindset to shift," Jamie said. "I want you to start thinking about your RRSPs not as a chunk of capital to be used to make investment decisions, but as your pensions—because that's what they are."

Meredith clued in. "So we *do* have pensions."

"Absolutely, Meredith. Your RRSPs are your pension plan and should be managed just like one."

"So the question is," I said, "how do pensions manage their assets?"

Jamie referred to the workbook Meredith and I had worked on before our much-needed vacation. He flipped to the section marked Personal and Financial Goals, the very section we had had so much difficulty completing. He highlighted one particular part of the page. "See this group of questions: When do you want to retire? and What will your expenses be?" Jamie asked.

"We had trouble with that one," I said.

"Most people do," Jamie said, "but it's an important concept. I assure you that the main preoccupation of pension managers is the future funding requirements of the pension's assets. They fret over asset mix and volatility for the sole outcome of accumulating sufficient assets to cover their required future cash outlays. In the same regard, we're attempting to create for you a nest egg that will function exactly like a pension—so we need to know what your personal future funding requirements are going to be."

Meredith was concerned. "And if we don't know yet exactly what our needs will be in retirement?"

"Then we use some rules of thumb," Jamie assured her. "I've made some assumptions that you'll see in the document: a retirement age of sixty-five and a need for about 75 percent of your existing income. Now, a pension plan uses an actuary to determine the rate of return that, coupled with the firm's ability to fund the plan, will grow the pension's existing assets to meet the plan's needs. We don't use an actuary, but we do use some complex software. I've determined that you need to grow your assets at 7 percent in order to meet your goals."

I looked over at Meredith and could see she was quite uncomfortable. She surprised me by putting the document down and looking seriously at Jamie. "Frankly, Jamie, I don't think there is any point in continuing until we resolve a few issues," she said.

Jamie responded, "You're absolutely right. I always want to have frank and open discussions with you. Tell me what's on your mind."

"During our discussions, some things came up that we need to address. For Pieter, the issue is a lack of confidence in the markets. He is sceptical of the notion that you just ask us some questions and plug our answers into a computer and somehow we get an asset mix that fulfills all our dreams."

"That's fair," Jamie replied.

"The second is more my issue. How can I cope with the volatility? I've never really liked the ups and downs, and I have to tell you, I do get very worried about it. Essentially, how confident can we be that we're going to get this 7-percent rate of return that's supposed to create the perfect pension?"

"Great questions," Jamie said. "Why don't I deal with them one at a time?"

I had to admit it myself: they were great questions. Meredith had hit on the two issues that had been bothering us. She had also set the tone of our meeting with Jamie; frankly, the news reports lately had not been very reassuring. I was interested in Jamie's take on things, not some magic solution to our problems.

"Let me attempt to deal with your issue first, Pieter," Jamie continued. "If I understand it, you're uncertain of our process and how it helps you meet your goals."

"No, I think the process sounds fine. It's the future of the markets I'm worried about. You've suggested that if we have the right asset mix, and we fund it correctly, everything will work out just fine," I replied.

"Basically, that's the idea," Jamie said.

"The problem I see is the markets. What if they don't co-operate? What if the economy sours? What if the increasing global problems persist for years? You have to admit things have never been this bad before."

Jamie smiled. I could tell he had heard this rant from other clients. "Look, Pieter, I don't want to disagree with your point of view, because it's important that we factor your perspective into our considerations of your risk tolerance. But let me give you my take on the markets. The investment market's future value will reflect the future value of the companies that make it up. I would suggest that the future can be predicted from the past." Jamie referred to one of the charts on the wall, a line graph charting the performance of various markets over a number of decades. "If you look closely at some of these time periods, you'll notice that, over long periods of time, the return on the various asset classes are, in fact, quite predictable and reliable. If you read Jeremy Siegel's *Stocks for the Long Run*, you'll discover that the markets have been performing very well for the last two hundred years, a time period that includes all kinds of wars, famine, depression and pestilence."

"And what if we have one devastating event that causes the market to crash again?" Meredith asked, sticking to one of her favourite themes.

"Andrew always reminds me that he was my age during the crash of 1987. The Dow Jones Industrial Average fell over five hundred points in one day, which was about 25 percent. Black Monday had an enormous emotional impact on the markets back then. Well, here it is on the graph—it's a blip. It turned out to be a short-term event, just like all the others."

"So you don't think things are worse today?" I asked.

"Let me tell you a story I heard this year. I was at an old friend's for dinner, and her older sister was visiting from the States with her husband, John. We were talking about the sad state of affairs in the world, and John told us what it was like when he was a child in the early sixties. His father was a leading rocket scientist for the government, and he and his family lived in the Washington, DC, area during the Cuban missile crisis. He and his older brother attended a private school in Virginia, outside the capital's blast zone. In both their lockers at school was a note with the address of relations out west in case Washington was hit by a nuclear weapon."

Jamie stopped and let his words sink in.

"That's quite a story," I responded.

"Those were tough times, Pieter. Kids used to do bomb drills even here in Canada. Many Canadians built bomb shelters in their basements. Don't believe the media. Things are not getting worse. I think they're getting better. The Cold War is over, and more and more countries are becoming democracies. Yes, there are many problems in the world. But the markets have survived them in the past, and they'll survive them in the future."

"It's funny," Meredith jumped in. "I hadn't thought about bomb drills in years. I remember my older siblings talking about them. Thinking back now, it's extraordinary that they had to put children through an exercise like that. Fortunately, they were too young to consider what the real implications were."

"The point is, Pieter, there is always unrest in the world, and we can't predict what's going to happen. But what I feel we *can* predict is the performance of the investment market over the long term, based on its history of reliability. Now for your concerns, Meredith. They are actually quite closely related to Pieter's issue. Remember, while the capital markets are very reliable over long periods of time, they're completely unpredictable over short periods of time. Unfortunately, I don't have a solution for you, just some comments for you to think about," Jamie replied.

"So you don't see volatility easing in the future?" Meredith asked.

"Actually, it's only going to get worse. We have greater numbers of middle-aged investors, they have a greater participation rate, and we have technology that allows for a greater volume of transactions. We also have an investment industry that has opened up access to the markets. It's a recipe for activity."

Meredith had an uneasy smile on her face—a smile that quickly faded. "That doesn't give me a whole lot of confidence."

"But we can ignore volatility if we have faith in the ultimate outcome. The key lies in how we control it for our purposes. If we have an excellent management system and we hold high-quality assets, then we have to have faith in where we will end up." Jamie said.

"And what's the basis for my faith?" Meredith asked.

"I think it's just like religious faith. Faith is being sure of what we hope for and certain of what we cannot see. The basis for most people's religious faith is found in historical evidence, personal experience or the personal experience of others they respect. Studies show that it's good for your well-being to believe, and there's a great body of evidence that people who connect with faith have greater stability. The markets have a great history. I believe the capitalist system has proven its worth, and the world's economies are improving. So ignore the short term, don't let the media throw you off, and focus on the task at hand."

I could see that Meredith was really thinking this one over. "Okay, we've spent enough time on this. I'll mull over what you've said. We can table this for now, but I want it to be a discussion-in-progress."

"Duly noted. Now let's look at your plan. What I can do is continue to address your concerns as we move through the data, so let me show you how we came up with a suggested asset mix. As I said, you need a 7-percent average rate of return. This translates into an asset mix of approximately 70 percent equities, 25 percent bonds, and 5 percent cash. If you look at the first page of the report I gave you, it will show you a pie chart of asset mix."

Meredith and I flipped open the document and had a look at the graph.

Jamie continued, "Equities are unreliable in the short term, yet provide the best returns in the long run, so they help hedge the risk that you will run out of money when you are seventy. Therefore, we invest only that portion of your money you won't need for five to ten years in equities. The value of this portion of your portfolio can bounce around as much as it likes in the short term. It's tough to take, Meredith, but irrelevant to your financial health. Bonds are more predictable over the medium term, so we invest money you will need over the next two to five years in bonds. The cash component has no risk in the short term, but huge long-term risk because of the erosion of purchasing power due to inflation. We use this component to meet your cash-flow requirements on a day-to-day basis."

"So, if we ever need money from our portfolio, and the market has just dropped 20 percent, we take it from the cash component, since it's unaffected, and let the market recover

over the next few years." I was actually starting to under-stand how money is managed!

"That's right, Pieter. Your asset mix policy also helps you take advantage of the volatility of the market by forcing you to rebalance your portfolio. Let's say your asset mix shifts to 60/35/5 because the market hits a bump. You're concerned about the market, and I'm concerned the new mix won't meet our targets. So we rebalance the 10-percent overage from bonds back into the market precisely at the time when it is opportune to buy—remember: buy low, sell high. There's a great Warren Buffett quote: 'Risk is not knowing what you are doing.' Meredith, I think you feel vulnerable because you've been guessing about what you should do next."

"I think that's right," Meredith replied. "I'm always wondering if we're doing the right thing."

"This asset mix method will empower you. We will always be moving, or rather rebalancing, in the right direc-tion," Jamie said.

"And what if the markets go down for a protracted period?" I asked.

"We have faith. We stick to our guns. We don't panic; we let common sense override our natural emotional reactions. And we use proper technique." Jamie paused, and I could almost see the light bulb switch on above his head. "I have a hockey story that may illustrate this point."

Sports stories are not generally Meredith's favourites, as we could see clearly from her grimace, but I was certainly keen.

"It's okay, Meredith. It'll be quick. This is about the 2003 playoff series between the Ottawa Senators and the

Philadelphia Flyers. Roman Cechmanek, the Flyers goal-tender, had an absolutely dismal series. After it was over, Don Cherry referred to him as a guesser, a goalie who, instead of relying on technique, tries to out-think the other team. Cherry's view was that you have to fire a goalie like that because the players in front of him lose heart. It's exactly like that with investing. If we use the proper techniques, we can have faith that we can get through the many rough spots in the markets. If we're just guessing, eventually we're going to get ourselves into trouble."

"That wasn't so bad. Actually, that analogy really does work," Meredith said.

"Then I'll continue to use it—I'm glad it occurred to me. Now we need to translate your investment goals into a working model. For this, we have a personalized Investment Policy Statement."

"So this is where the rubber meets the road?" I asked.

"This is it. This document defines how and what we do. You have a template for it in the package I gave you earlier. Why don't you take a minute to look it over?"

Meredith and I turned the page in the document we were holding and saw a list of ten items:

1. Statement of purpose: Outlines expectations and objectives for Investment Policy (Mission Statement).
2. Definition of roles and responsibilities: Defines job descriptions or roles of all participants.
3. Documentation: Itemizes all documents relevant to the plan.
4. Investment goals and risk parameters: Outlines target returns and risk guidelines for all assets.

5. Asset allocation policy: States target ranges for all asset classes and rebalance policy to adhere to target mix.
6. Policy constraints: Determines and lists assets that will not be part of the mix.
7. Cash flow: States cash-flow requirements (short- and long-term, and strategy to secure these).
8. Due diligence: Outlines manager criteria for asset selection.
9. Reporting criteria: Lists both internal and external reporting criteria.
10. Review and valuation: Sets formal dates to rebalance and review asset mix and investment performance.

Meredith and I took a moment to digest it all. The list was a little daunting. "I guess it was easier when someone just told me what to buy," I said, only half joking.

"I know it looks lengthy, but we have to set up our process at the beginning and stick to it. Again, it acts as our guide through good markets and bad," Jamie replied.

"And once your clients set this process up, are they generally good at sticking to it?" Meredith asked.

"To be honest, Meredith, it varies," Jamie said. "Some people struggle with change, and some will always revert back to old habits. The key for us as advisors is that the policy statement gives us a context for the plan we are trying to deliver. It gives us a fighting chance to keep our clients on track, because it helps them avoid picking investments on the fly."

It made a lot of sense to me, even if the work seemed to be highly front-end loaded. Deep down, the process appealed to the engineer in me, which craved order and discipline.

"A specific process also makes it easy for you when you're performing a personal audit," Jamie said.

"A personal audit?" Meredith asked. "What's that?"

"Well, as part of your annual review, you may want to assess how well you're meeting your goals. Many of our clients evaluate all the aspects of their lives, finances being merely one."

"That makes a lot of sense," I said. "Everything fits together."

"It sure does," Jamie replied. "And for a whole lot of Canadians, the clock is ticking. They're reaching that age when they need to get it right."

"That's exactly our mindset," Meredith said.

"Okay, all of this sounds logical, but the one thing I'm unclear about is execution," I said. "How do we go about investing our money?"

Jamie had taken us through a rather exhaustive planning exercise. We had begun to get into the habit of discussing what we wanted from our lives, and we were starting to understand the advantages of asset mix and investment policy and process. But I was still unsure how to pull off the final step.

"To be honest, I'm a little unclear on how you want to proceed," Jamie responded. "You see, there are a few investment styles and options you could choose."

"And you'll let us choose what we feel is best?" I asked.

"You'll choose, but in the end that choice will determine whether you'll deal with Andrew and me. We believe quite adamantly that you need to pick a means to your end and stick with it," Jamie replied.

"And what would you recommend?" I asked.

"I'm going to leave that for Andrew to tell you when he meets with you. But I'll review what I believe are the three distinct methods you could choose," Jamie said.

"Are there only three?" Meredith asked.

"There are many variations, but I think these three cover your options at this point. First off, you could go the traditional route and self-direct your investments. If you do, I believe you have to be involved in all aspects of your investment decisions. You need to work intimately with your advisor and be prepared to react to the advice you're given. You need to make sure you have a common view of the investment markets, and you have to be willing to take the time to understand the research you're given and respond. And, perhaps most importantly, you have to take responsibility for your actions."

"Sounds a little daunting," Meredith said.

"Not for some people, but you need to know what you're doing and what you're trying to accomplish. The second option is becoming popular. It's a scaled-down variation of the self-directed approach. All of the major advisory firms have created model portfolios for clients. Using the skills of their analysts, they have built portfolios to suit different risk tolerances. Clients retain their own portfolio of stocks and allow the pros to advise them on when to make a switch. These accounts are fee-based, so if your advisor recommends that you alter positions, you can feel sure the advice is not based on transaction costs."

"That sounds like an interesting way to go," I replied. "Almost like a compromise on what we were doing before."

"That sounds right. Now, the third option is to completely give up day-to-day control to a group of pension managers. All the assets, based on a prescribed mix, are managed by professionals with different criteria of both investment style and risk tolerance. These accounts are designed, for all intents and purposes, to give you the experience that Canadians with a pension have."

"That sounds intriguing," Meredith said.

"I'm not so sure," I argued. "Giving up complete control is something I'd like to think about."

"And that's what you should do. Take your financial plan home and read through it. Andrew will want to meet with you in a few days, and he can discuss our approach and the reasons behind it."

"You don't want to tell us now?" I laughed.

"Andrew has a lot of experience, and he can take you through the evolution of our management style. Remember, it's best that both parties feel comfortable up front," Jamie replied.

We gathered up our financial planning documents. It had been a rigorous two hours, but I was starting to understand the importance of labouring over process before investing our money. No more ready-shoot-aim.

11
Majoring in Minor Things

RUTH

Early on a summer Sunday morning, I woke up thinking about Meredith. I worry about her. She talks a good game, but I'm just not sure she gets it. So I decided to act on my worry. Rather than ruminate about Meredith, I phoned her when the clock struck ten (I figured that's when you can properly phone someone on a Sunday morning) and arranged to have a quick coffee with her at eleven at the Starbucks on the main street that runs down the middle of our neighbourhood. Coffee shops aren't my favourite places in the world, but when you don't feel like tidying your own house to receive guests, they sure make marvellous locales to meet friends.

Meredith was keen for the diversion a trip to Starbucks offered. She'd been planning to mow the lawn, but decided she'd give that task to Emily and meet me instead.

As I got ready to go, I sorted through the source of my worries. Over the past few weeks, I've been listening to her talk about the work she and Pieter have been doing to order their financial affairs. She's told me about the sessions they've had with Jamie. Our conversations on the topic always circle back to her concern about certainty. Actually, they're more about her fear of lack of certainty.

Meredith doesn't like the great unknowns that life tends to place in everyone's path. Her current worry is the volatility of the stock market. Despite reassurances, she still doesn't trust that it will deliver what she needs, when she needs it. But if it isn't one thing, she'll find something else to worry about. She'll worry about whether Malcolm is eating right at university, whether she'll find another contract after we're finished our book, whether Emily will pass chemistry.

For me, one of the wonderful bonuses about being an "older" adult is the evaporation of worry. I know I can cope with what life throws at me. I know my potential. I know I'll survive the slings and arrows that occur on a regular basis in everyone's life. I know I can't control what will happen to others. I'm no longer a worrier. But Meredith is not quite there yet.

I see so much of myself—my much younger self—in Meredith. I remember the days of rushing to pick up Dylan at daycare, speeding home to cook a meal, hurrying through homework and bedtime routines, all the while hoping to catch a minute or two for myself along the way. I know that having all those balls in the air at one time tends to breed anxiety and make the unknowns seem larger and scarier than they really are. Would it be so horrible if Emily failed chemistry or Malcolm survived on Kraft Dinner for a month? Meredith needs to learn to look at her worries and size them up for what they really are.

I decided that, this Sunday morning, I would remind her that this chapter of her life will soon have sped by and that, soon enough, she will have the time she wants for herself, her goals and her plans. Soon enough, she will have a slower life if she wants it and will be able to indulge her own passions. Soon enough, she will realize that many of her biggest worries were totally ungrounded—a complete waste of her valuable time.

I know that, intellectually, she understands that she needs a more manageable pace of life. On the phone the other day, we discussed *In Praise of Slow*, the book by Carl Honoré that Hazen lent her a few weeks back. According to Honoré, demographics are on the side of deceleration. We've talked about including this theme in our book. Over the next couple of decades, as populations age across the developed world, our societies will be slowing down.

It's one thing to analyze something about society as a whole, but it's quite another to be caught up in the tornado of one's own life. Meredith can't truly anticipate her future. But whether she decides to slow down is her choice—a change she will make in her own life. I can't impose it on her, no matter how much I think she might need it.

I kept this thought firmly in my head as I walked toward Starbucks: If she's going to change, it must come from within. I can only support her by giving her my thoughts and information. I can't change Meredith. That's her task.

When I turned the corner, I saw her. Starbucks was already bustling with people, but she'd snagged us a table on the patio that fronts the coffee shop. She was unloading an armful of books from a canvas bag onto the table. I guessed she figured I'd arranged this meeting to talk about our work on the book.

I decided not to rush into a heavy discussion with Meredith. Like Uncle Jack used to say, "A wise man knows what he says, a fool says what he knows." I didn't want to challenge Meredith and make her feel uncomfortable, I just wanted to make her think.

"Hey, I'm buying this morning," I said, putting my arm around Meredith and giving her a hug.

"That suits me perfectly. I haven't had a chance to get to the bank machine, and I'm cleaned out," Meredith replied. "Emily asked for a handout last night."

"I remember those days. Dylan was always looking for a few bucks to go to a movie or buy a coffee."

"As a matter of fact, that's exactly what Emily did: she went to a movie with a group of girlfriends, and they ended up right here at Starbucks. As I left her mowing the lawn, she told me I need to try a Caramel Macchiato."

"Okay—I can do that for you."

When I emerged from the shop with a tray loaded with cups and scones, Meredith pushed the books to one side of the table, thanked me and picked up the book on the top of the stack. "I loved *In Praise of Slow*," she said, opening the book to a place she'd marked with a yellow sticky note. "We're really the authors of our own fate. Let me read you this: 'Recent generations have been reared to believe it is their right and duty to have it all: family, career, house, rewarding social life. But "having it all" has turned out to be a poisoned chalice.' Honoré then goes on to say that women are particularly eager for work-life balance. They're fed up with being frazzled and are working to change the rules of the workplace."

So far, so good. I decided to keep things on the impersonal side to start. I figured if we eased into the conversation, we'd get to the personal details of Meredith's life soon enough. "We've talked about this before," I said. "It's all a matter of balance. On one hand, you've got nearly 80 percent of Canadians who rank maintaining a good, stable marriage as the most or second-most important priority in their lives, and then you look at statistics about working hours. Back in the early nineties, one in ten Canadians worked more than fifty hours per week. Now that's up to one in four. Something's got to give. There aren't enough hours in the day to work like that and then devote quality time to developing a great marriage and family life. You can't have it all," I replied.

"I've been thinking about that a lot this past week," Meredith said, pulling another book from her stack. "I've been reading *Status Anxiety*, by Alain de Botton. It's about how nearly all of us share an anxiety about what others think of us. How we're measured by what we have. We're a success if we have a lot of stuff, a failure if we don't. He writes about how wealth is not an absolute. Here, listen to this: wealth 'is relative to desire. Every time we yearn for something we cannot afford, we grow poorer, whatever our resources. And every time we feel satisfied with what we have, we can be counted as rich, however little we may actually possess.'"

"Uncle Jack had a saying that summarizes that fact rather neatly: 'As the wallet grows, so do the needs.'"

"Precisely. But I hadn't thought of it exactly that way before reading *Status Anxiety*. The more you have, the more you want. And that's why, according to the author, Americans spend more time at the mall than anywhere but the workplace or home. I think I'm a bit caught up in status anxiety, and that's why I'm so worried about our financial planning. I don't want to look and feel like a loser in a world of winners because Pieter and I don't end up really comfortable in our retirement."

It hadn't taken long for the conversation to tip into the personal realm. This was going to be easier than I thought. Meredith was already thinking through many of the things that concerned me. "This is so strange. I've been thinking of talking to you about precisely this. *The Christian Science Monitor* reported recently that the average person in the United States now does the equivalent of a month more work in a year than they did in the 1970s—that's got to take a toll on a person, and on marriage and family life. We work for a lot of reasons, but one of the key ones is to make more money so that we can keep up with the Joneses. And we make ourselves anxious about the unknown by focusing on things that are beyond our control, and those are not the real things that make us happy in the long run."

"The author talks about that in *Status Anxiety*. He says that the greater the number of people we compare ourselves to, the more there will be for us to envy," she replied, flipping quickly to another yellow sticky note. "He quotes Chamfort: 'Nature didn't tell me: "Don't be poor." Nor indeed: "Be rich." But she does beg me: "Be independent."' And that's exactly what I want Pieter and me to be—independent and happy. So far, our greatest happiness comes from our marriage and our family."

"I read some interesting statistics recently on marriage in Canada. Canadians are marrying later than ever—if they do marry. In their twenties, young Canadians are dating, maybe trying out a joint living arrangement. Between 1995 and 2001, the number of couples living common-law rose by 20 percent, while the number of married couples increased by just 3 percent."

"Wow, that's a big change in a short period of time."

"Attitudes change, and we need to be aware of those changes. The average age of brides and grooms in this country is now into the thirties. In 2000, on average, brides were nearly thirty-two and grooms slightly over thirty-four."

"Sounds like people have cold feet about marriage."

"Here's the interesting thing. Canadians might be putting marriage off until they're older, but they seem to be very happy they've taken the plunge. Ipsos Canada conducted a poll in 2003 that showed that only one in seven Canadians wished at some point to just wake up one morning and not be married anymore. That means approximately 85 percent of married Canadians have never thought this. By and large, Canadians are content in their marriages, and that translates into good things over the long haul."

"Yes, I just read something in the newspaper about happiness. A new study out of the University of Texas shows that happy, satisfied people have a significantly better chance of staying stronger and more mobile as they age than those who are unhappy. I clipped it, thinking it might be something we could use in our book. But it also made me think: 'Be happy.'"

We laughed and sat for a moment, watching the world go by, sipping our coffees. Buses rumbled down the street. A kid rolled by on a two-wheeler with training wheels, his mother walking behind him. An elderly woman pushed her shopping cart. Two teenage girls walked a frisky golden retriever. A dad strolled by with a baby in a Snugli.

I figured I'd talked enough about generalities. It was time to get to Meredith's specific situation. "So, how are you going to achieve independence and happiness?" I asked, taking a sip of my coffee.

"Well, through planning, for one. And we're already started on that, working with Jamie to plan our finances. Then there are a few other things. Accepting that I can't control everything around me. Understanding that I'm at a stage in my life where I'm probably the busiest I'll ever be. Looking at my life as a long, hopefully happy and healthy continuum. And—finally—calming down and enjoying the ride."

"I have some ideas about a couple of the items on your list. You talk about accepting that you can't control every last detail. That's very true. But it's easy to say, hard to do. I don't want to force anything on you, but can I tell you how I work at dealing with uncertainty?"

Meredith nodded her head. "Please do."

"First, I don't let myself become Chicken Little. When I face a potential problem, my first inclination is to make it way bigger than it actually is. I always pull myself back from the brink of 'the sky is falling' and chart out a practical response to cut the problem down to size. Second, I always try to think ahead. Someone with a plan is always better prepared to cope with uncertain situations. Even if your plan has to change as a result of something unforeseen, you'll have the skill of strategizing that comes from developing plans, and that skill will come in handy. Finally, I always remind myself that I've faced problems in the past and conquered them by staying calm, thinking things through and focusing on what I can control, not on details I have no ability to change."

I could see that Meredith was receptive to my approach. She was nodding, listening intently, head tipped slightly to one side. Funny, she'd heard it all before, but now she seemed ready to really hear it and act upon it.

I waited a couple of seconds before launching into round two. "You're right: you're at one of the busiest junctures of your life. You're no different, really, than any other boomer woman your age. Life seems to layer on busyness. The question is, Why are you so busy? Your early years of consumption and lots of it are behind you. You've got your house and cottage—both nicely furnished. And yet you're still spending lots of money."

"You saw the state of my wallet this morning. My kids are amazingly expensive these days, what with Malcolm at university and Emily not far behind. They do contribute a bit with their jobs. Em was so excited when she came home with her first paycheque from the Body Shop. I think I took the wind out of her sails a bit when I told her Pieter and I expected her to save a portion of it for university. Still, we shell out incredible amounts of money for them."

"It seems to me that's one of the major sources of your anxiety about the future. Will you have enough money to fund your retirement? You're staring your fifties in the face, and you're thinking about the years beyond middle age. What do they hold—and not just financially, but physically, personally?"

"Okay, here's the message I'm going to take from our conversation today. Plan for the future, but live in the present. I can't control the future, I can only prepare for it. With the work Pieter and I have been doing with Jamie, I'm doing that on the financial front. We will have enough money to support the kids through school, then look after our own needs. With the work I'm doing with you and Hazen, I'm doing that on the career front. With the relationships I have with my family and friends, I'm doing that on the personal front. And you may not know this yet, Ruth, but you and I have enrolled in a Pilates class at the Y. So that's a start at taking care of the physical side of things."

I hoisted my coffee cup. "Here's to you, Meredith. It looks like you've got your bases covered. And you're looking after me too! Now relax!"

"Look, Ruth," she replied. "I'm not as dumb as I look. I'm going to quote your Uncle Jack back to you: 'A wise man hears one word and understands two.' Don't think I don't know that when you talk generally about the baby boomers, then intersperse your worldly wisdom into the conversation, we're talking about more than the book we're writing, we're talking about your worries about me."

She was on to me! Well, as Uncle Jack always said, honesty is the best policy. "You're absolutely right," I admitted. "But, here's the thing. I started out the morning being worried, but listening to you today, I see you've taken things in hand. You're on your way, Meredith, and I'm proud of you."

"Okay, okay. Thanks for the compliment. But before this turns all mushy, I have something I think we absolutely need to include in our book." She pulled a file folder out of her canvas bag and opened it to a collection of photocopied articles. "Did you know the first National

Convention of the Idle was held in a little Italian village this summer?" she asked.

"Sounds like something I should have attended."

"Okay—that's precisely the reaction I expected from you. You know there's nothing wrong with sitting around for a bit and enjoying your life."

"Exactly."

"This is a great fit with the thesis of *In Praise of Slow*. Just let me tell you how the BBC reported on the convention. 'Do nothing' was the theme of the event. Participants were told that idle people find smart ways to get the same results with less effort. The symbol of the movement is the hammock, and idleness is touted as the elixir of long life in a world of deadlines."

"I love it," I said. "And this story fits perfectly with my comments about what not to worry about. You know, I think we fill our time with too many useless chores that make for stress and worry. We all need to recognize that we can't be perfect. So why not stop on a Sunday morning— enjoy coffee with a friend rather than heading to the grocery store to find the perfect ingredients for a brunch for twelve, with the perfect floral arrangement and table setting. Take a load off."

In response, Meredith scooped up the books and file folder and placed them all back in her bag. "I guess we'll finish this conversation on Monday when I come over to your place to work with you and Hazen."

That's what I like about this woman, I thought. She's a quick study.

12
Size Matters—It Just Does

PIETER

Planning our financial future had certainly been a long and careful process. Meredith and I had had meetings with Jamie and numerous discussions on our own, and now we were meeting with Andrew Proctor, Jamie's senior partner. But even now, it would be foolish to think we had things completely figured out and were ready to start investing, full speed ahead. I'm sure Jamie and Andrew proceed at this pace to force us to think our goals and objectives through thoroughly.

The process we were now considering was the polar opposite of our past experiences. We didn't dwell then on the importance of our investments to our future well-being. But after a few false starts, it was imperative that we get it right this time.

I had spoken with Andrew at some length to get a general sense of what to expect at our meeting with him. He gave me a rough agenda and stressed that his role was quite different from Jamie's. In fact, we all had roles to play in our relationship with Andrew's firm. Step one—the life plan—was for Meredith and me to hash out on our own. As both Jamie and Andrew had independently confirmed, they were happy to help us execute our goals and aspirations, but it was up to us to dream. Step two—the financial plan—was Jamie's domain. He had worked with our future plans to create an actionable strategy that would help us achieve them. Step three—investment planning—was where Andrew came in.

Andrew was quite humorous on the phone when he described how he and Jamie work together. Andrew called Jamie his "numbers guy," and conceded it was not his favourite part of the process. He feels strongly that the latter two elements of the plan should be managed by people with different skill sets. He believes he and Jamie work so well together because they have very different abilities.

Jamie was going to sit in on our meeting with Andrew, and I was happy about that—it would give us some continuity. Meredith and I arrived at eleven, and Jamie came out and greeted us. Andrew was just finishing up a conference call, and he joined us a minute later. He showed us into his office and got down to business.

"So the planning process with Jamie has been moving along well?" he asked, clearly looking for feedback.

"It's been extremely helpful," Meredith replied. "I think we have a much better sense not only of what we need to think about but also of the importance of a planning process."

"You'll find that everything we do is driven by a specific process, whether it's executing a financial plan or implementing an investment mix. I have advised clients for more than two decades. I've seen the good, the bad and the very bad. In the end, investing can be more predictable if we set policy guidelines and stick to them."

Meredith and I settled in, and Andrew gave us an overview of what he wanted to talk about during the meeting. "Today I want to give you a sense of how we would execute your plan and manage your money going forward. As I said, I've been doing this for some time, and our process has evolved into the program I'll describe. Over the years, I've watched hundreds of investors both thrive and struggle in the markets. As a result, I know what works—and I also have a good feel for what doesn't."

"You may recall that at our last meeting I reviewed the existing strategies you could pursue," Jamie said.

"Yes, the three different management techniques," I responded. "Meredith and I have discussed them, but, frankly, we are still up in the air about what we should do."

"That's fine," Andrew said. "I want to briefly discuss the issues we think you face and tell you our recommended strategy. This may fit with your views, and it may not. One thing is critical, and I want to emphasize this point: whichever direction or style you choose, you have to be committed to it."

"I guess that has been one of our weaknesses in the past," Meredith replied.

"Uncertainty is a killer in the markets," Andrew said. "Jamie and I have reviewed some of the concerns you raised. I believe your worries about volatility, Meredith, stem from not understanding the process. If we are clear where we're headed and how we are getting there, we can overcome the obstacles that will inevitably be put in our way."

Meredith nodded. Andrew continued, "Your concerns about the future of the markets, Pieter, are a little more difficult to address. I could compare the faith I have in the markets to faith in a higher power, but that's probably not going to cut it."

"That might be a bit of a stretch," I said.

"Okay, then let's stick with the facts. Let me quickly show you two graphs that demonstrate why I'm so optimistic about the future. Now, remember, the stock market is a reflection of our wealth and economic well-being. If we're doing well, the economy grows and real estate goes up, and the stock markets reflect this with higher valuations."

"Makes sense," I responded.

"I know you've worked with Hazen, Meredith, so this data should come as no surprise to you. This research was put together recently by one of the large banking institutions in Canada." Andrew handed us two sheets of paper each and continued. "Now, the first graph shows our collective savings rates at different ages. It's quite clear that our ability to save and invest starts to peak as we hit our mid-fifties."

"It makes sense," Meredith said. "That's when we have the capacity and the motivation to do so."

"Exactly. The boomers have just begun to enter their mid-fifties. Between the ages of fifty-five and sixty-five, the average Canadian has a personal savings rate of over 15 percent, double what they had a decade earlier. This is also about the time that earnings peak, so the amounts they have to save and invest should be very encouraging." Andrew paused to drink some coffee, then continued. "This second graph is even more exciting. It's a quiet trend that's going to have enormous implications for the markets. This graph projects total assets versus total liabilities for Canadian households over the next two decades. Pieter, I think one of the reasons you're concerned about the markets is the media's obsession with bad news. I'm sure you've read many articles about the debt crisis. What you haven't read about is the explosion of assets at a much greater pace. Such data predict that over the next fifteen years household assets will almost double, while liabilities will remain relatively unchanged. That's a debt-to-equity ratio performance any company would be pleased to have."

"You're right on two counts—we do get a lot of bad news, and I hadn't heard anything about the explosion of assets," I said.

"News does affect the market," Andrew replied, "but only for a very brief time. Economic fundamentals affect the market over longer periods and, frankly, looking at these graphs, our future looks tremendous."

"Okay, I feel better," I responded, looking over at Meredith, who looked thoughtful as she took all this in. Andrew probably had her convinced as soon as he mentioned the aging population. Hazen must have tipped him off on her interest in boomer demographics.

"Good, because a positive outlook is enormously helpful as we try to deal with the highs and lows of the investment world," Andrew replied.

"We will try to be positive in the future," I said, and both Meredith and I laughed.

"Okay, let's move on to the execution of your plan. It's my belief that, when you break it down, there are really only two types of investors in the marketplace today," Andrew said.

"Only two?" I asked, a little dubious about this statement.

"Perhaps 'investor mindsets' would be a more appropriate term. We characterize investors as either 'absolute return' or 'relative return' investors," Andrew replied. He stood up, walked over to an easel with blank flipchart paper on it, and drew two large inverted T's. The top one he labelled "absolute return" and the bottom one "relative return." "The first chart is an example of an absolute return investor. These are people who self-direct and attempt to make a maximum rate of return." Andrew took his marker and put random dots all over the top graph.

"That would describe what we've been doing," I responded.

"You and about 90 percent of investors," Andrew replied. "In effect, they're trying to outperform the market. There are two problems with this approach: the random nature of returns and the investor's reaction to the wide range of outcomes this method of investing will inevitably produce. 'The random nature of returns' is just another way of saying volatility. This is what you've struggled with, Meredith. The centre line represents the market. When we're to the right of it, we are overperforming. The common reaction here is, 'This is great, let's get more.' When we're over to the left, we feel stressed and fret over what to do next. It's fear and greed, in graphic display."

"And the other method would reduce these problems?" Meredith asked.

"'Reduce' is the right word, because this process certainly won't eliminate them. Relative returns is basically a technique that advocates tracking the market." Andrew put a number of dots on the lower graph, all close to the centre line. "As I will show you in a moment, investors try way too hard to beat the market. If only they understood that, given the tremendous consistency of market returns, all they have to do is find a way to match the market. By diversifying and attempting to cover market returns, we reduce risk and volatility—and hopefully some of our uneasiness."

"It's almost like the first-date experience: don't try too hard; just be yourself," I said.

"That's not a bad analogy," Andrew replied.

Meredith gave me a surprised look. Even after twenty years of marriage, I can still amaze her with my masculine sensitivity. Not bad for an engineer!

Andrew continued, "Absolute return methodology, while initially favoured by a large majority, will quickly reveal its challenges as you try to successfully execute it. This is what you are really doing when you self-direct, and it is my strong belief that the average investor lacks the temperament, know-how, patience and will to be consistently successful as markets bounce around."

"I think Pieter and I have found that out the hard way. It always seemed so easy when the markets were doing well. Then they'd shift, and the trouble would start," Meredith said.

"Let me show you research results from some institutions that study how the general public fares. These first two are perhaps the most devastating," Andrew handed us a couple of bar graphs that demonstrated different rates of return. "Now, the first one you're looking at is stock market data from the U.S. markets for the years 1984 through 2000. This period represents the great bull market. What you see is that the average equity mutual fund produced a 13.1-percent return. The average holder of these funds, however, produced a 5.3-percent return."

"How is that possible?" I asked. "Shouldn't their performance be identical?"

"It would be, but investors tried to time the market. In a nutshell, they attempted to attain an absolute performance. Do you know how good it is if you can compound your money at a rate above 10 percent? But by trying too hard, investors created a negative performance gap of almost 8 percent."

"I see that the next graph shows a similar situation here in Canada," Meredith said.

"The dates are a little different," Andrew said. "The Canadian data is for the decade ending in 2002. But, yes, the results are similar: average mutual fund performance just below 8 percent; average fund holder below 5 percent—again, an enormous performance gap. It's the attempt to guess that causes the problem, because we are not making decisions from a position of strength."

"Here's an interesting one." Jamie handed us another study. "This is work done by one of the large fund companies, Templeton."

"It looks a little like the periodic table of the elements we studied back in high school," I joked.

"That's what I thought when I first saw it," Jamie replied. "It actually illustrates the eight different asset classes you could have invested in over the past twenty years. It includes bonds, small cap stocks, large cap stocks; Canadian, U.S. and international stocks. They are ranked each year by performance, best to worst, for the years 1981 to 2001."

"So they show what you could have invested in each year," I said.

"Exactly. Then Templeton had some fun with the data, and here's what they found. If, each year, you invested $10,000 in the top performer from the previous year—which, by the way, about 90 percent of the public does—you ended the twenty years with $600,000, or a 9.6-percent rate of return."

"That sounds like our strategy," I replied.

"Wait for it," Jamie said. "Here's the fun part. If you chased the worst asset from the previous year, you ended up with $625,000."

"Isn't *that* interesting," Meredith responded.

Jamie smiled. "It gets better. If you spread your capital evenly across the asset classes, you finished with $745,000, an 11.3-percent rate of return. And if you rebalanced once a year and began each new year with your asset classes evenly distributed, you ended up with $765,000, or 11.6 percent."

"So by diversifying and rebalancing instead of chasing the hot sector, investors could have earned $165,000 more over twenty years. That's pretty compelling," I said.

"It certainly gives us a great reason to create a very specific approach to investing and stick with it," Andrew said. "What I'm hoping these charts illustrate is why it's so important to avoid ad hoc decisions." He paused for a moment and looked at us seriously. "But there is something even more profound in this data that goes to the very heart of human nature and the relationship between investors and their advisors. It's clear that we'd be better off investing in last year's loser than in last year's winner. But how many advisors would be successful if they offered that advice to clients? We'd be even better off if we diversified across the board, but Canadians have shown a propensity to chase the hot fund. How open are they to advice to steer clear of that approach?"

"This is what you meant about needing to see eye to eye with your advisor. We need to believe in the process," I said.

"It's so important," Andrew replied.

"It must get tough when clients start to head off in a direction their advisor doesn't believe in."

"I think it ends the relationship," Andrew said. "The final point I'll make on this data is that it took twenty years to play out. The average investor has about eighteen months of patience. They need a long-term plan so they don't make rash decisions after those eighteen months.

"Okay, enough of the background for why we invest the way we do. Let me show you how our process works. If you recall the different styles Jamie reviewed, we favour the approach that delegates finances to the experts. We believe you should run your life and the experts in the investment world should run your financial affairs. As you've learned, the market can be a tough place. We need to have a diversified, unemotional approach that performs well in all types of markets. Essentially, we need to create a pension for you."

"So this is how we deal with the problem that neither of us participates in a company pension?" I asked.

"That's right," Andrew replied. "Now, the reason you two met with Jamie first is that we want our clients to get a full appreciation for how the process works. Too many investors in Canada come racing into the market, often when it's hot, and make a mess of it because they have no real process at all."

"If you recall, this all started with a simple question: What are you doing in the market?" Jamie said. "We want to give our clients the ability to understand what they need to accomplish. Then they can use the market to help them accomplish those goals—nothing more."

"Okay, folks, here's where we get specific about your investment strategy." Andrew handed me a document that read Investment Policy Statement and explained that it was an addendum to the policy statement we had received from Jamie. "This is our business plan. Jamie and I have looked at all the data we have received from you. We've determined your tolerance for risk. We've looked at your long-term financial objectives, and from this we've established a target asset mix and a target rate of return. These are critical elements to your success. Investors are always surprised to learn that stock selection is somewhat unimportant but asset mix is crucial. In this document, you'll see the different pension managers we'll employ to manage your money."

"So no more picking stocks?" I asked.

"Not in our plan," Andrew replied. "We're going to delegate all asset management to these professionals around the world. Our job is to focus on the financial plan, and from it determine your investment policy to attain your goals. No more guessing."

"There's one thing that's troubling me," Meredith said. "I've been reading a number of articles lately about the dire outlook for many large pension funds."

"That's a fantastic point, Meredith, and it goes to the very heart of why we want to emulate the behaviour of *specific* pension funds," Andrew replied. "The pensions that find themselves in trouble are almost always those that are tied to a publicly traded stock. That is to say, the pensions of publicly traded companies. They are in trouble because they've made the same mistakes that smaller investors make: they concentrate too much on their own stock, a very risky strategy, and they often take a funding holiday from their annual contribution requirements when the markets have had a good run, assuming, I guess, that it will continue," Andrew responded.

"And it never does," I said.

"No, Pieter, even if the cycle is as long as it was in the nineties, it corrects eventually. The solution we always suggest is: act like a teacher," Andrew said.

"A teacher?" Meredith and I asked at the same time.

"You see, *there's* a pension we want to emulate. Teachers start a pension on their first day of work, and it's funded from every paycheque after that. They have excellent management of the assets, which the teachers themselves have nothing to do with. They have excellent diversification, and each teacher receives yearly projections on retirement dates and amounts. I can't imagine a better strategy than to try to reproduce a teacher's pension."

"And that's what you do?" Meredith asked.

"That's what we do," Andrew replied. He leaned over and handed me a list. "We focus on five key points that I'm certain lead to success for the average investor."

I scanned the list, then handed it to Meredith:

1. Create a specific written plan.
2. Focus on realistic goals and objectives.
3. Generate an asset mix policy sensitive to risk tolerance.
4. Establish a diversification and rebalancing strategy.
5. Focus on a long-term investment process.

"Because the market can be so volatile, we need a written plan, and we need to stick to it. It's really as simple as that," Andrew continued.

"And how does the process actually work?" Meredith asked.

"Why don't I let Jamie handle this," Andrew said. "I've spoken enough already."

"It's actually fairly straightforward once we set it up," Jamie replied. "Your policy statement allocates your capital to the different pension managers we employ. We tend to use about a dozen, with a wide range of styles. We'll have a rebalancing review with you every three months, and we'll have a more in-depth annual meeting at which we'll do a complete review of asset mix, risk tolerance and goals and objectives. Things change, and we should update information regularly."

"Sounds like a logical approach," I replied.

"We weren't kidding—engineers like it," Andrew replied. He paused and then continued. "There's one last thought I want to leave you with, and, again, it relates to pensions. The good pension managers know you have to fund pensions properly and there are no shortcuts to success. You can't hope for a hot market to fix your bad decisions. We always need to be mindful of the two risks we face in life."

"And they are?" I inquired.

"The risk of living too short a life, and the risk of living too long. The first risk is managed through insurance. The second we manage through savings. You need enough capital to have a good long retirement. Size matters—it just does. A savings strategy is crucial. Investors who start saving relatively late in life are often attracted to shortcuts. Unfortunately, many Canadians believe they can overcome a small savings account with an aggressive investment strategy. Perhaps this works for a few, but not many, I suspect. In the end, the right process and proper funding are the real keys to success."

"Your job now is to go home and think everything over," Jamie added. "If this process makes sense to you, then we have the basis to move forward, and we can give you a precise breakdown of asset mix. But it may not, and that's okay too. We just need to make sure up front that we have an understanding. Otherwise, you'll need to continue your search for an advisor, and hopefully our work will have helped you on your way to finding a solution for your financial affairs."

If nothing else, we were certainly learning a great deal about the challenges of investing. Meredith and I thanked Jamie and Andrew for their time and the amount of work they had done on our behalf. As we headed for the door, I knew we had a lot to discuss. I still had that time-is-running-out feeling, but I didn't want to make another mistake.

13
Golf, the Ultimate Guide for Investing

HAZEN

I really can't remember if I've ever looked forward to a game of golf more. We were playing, of course, first thing in the morning. Andrew had said on the phone that he'd heard you do your best thinking in the morning, after a good night's sleep. At my age, I'm up early, so it was fine by me.

When I got to the club, Andrew, true to form, was standing beside the green, chipping.

"It seems this is where I always find you, practising your short game," I said as I walked up.

"It's the most important part of the game, but I'll get to that later," he responded.

"So, what is our plan of action this morning?" I asked, pulling out my putter and rolling a few balls somewhat near the hole.

"I've spent some time on a little speech I call 'everything you need to know about investing you can learn on the golf course.' To be honest, I don't really know what to do with it. I may put it in a small book and give it to my clients. I appreciate you letting me try it out on you this morning," Andrew replied.

"So it's a comparison of golf and investing?" I asked.

"It's really a comparison of the frustrations we endure in both golf and investing," Andrew said. "As I got back into playing this game over the past few years, it struck me how much a knowledge of golf could contribute to an understanding of investing."

"There are a lot of people, especially boomers, who play golf, so that makes a lot of sense. If you give investors a frame of reference they can relate to, they might better appreciate what they're up against." I said.

"That's exactly it," Andrew replied. "And the more time I spent thinking about it, the more I realized how much the two activities have in common. As you well know, golf can make you crazy. And, of course, the markets can often have a similar effect."

This really was going to be entertaining. As we wandered down to the first tee, I told Andrew I was happy to be the test audience for his idea.

"I've arranged these ideas to coincide with this golf course. I came up with eighteen similarities between investing and golf," Andrew said.

"One idea per hole."

"Exactly," Andrew responded. "Some are fairly short ideas, which we'll discuss on the par threes. Some are a little more involved, and I've saved those for the par fives."

"And this first hole is a par five, so we open with a larger concept?" I asked.

"We open with, I believe, the most difficult concept. Both golf and investing are counterintuitive." Andrew let his opening salvo sink in as we lined up our drives. Then, as we wandered down the fairway, he continued. "Think about it. With golf, you have to hit down to make the ball go up. If you swing harder, the ball generally doesn't go as far. The higher the number on the club, the shorter the distance the ball travels. It's hard to convince yourself to do what you need to do to be successful."

I smiled. "And if you start to get annoyed, you naturally try to swing harder, and that never works." I hunted around for my ball, which, typically, had landed in the rough.

"Of course not. Now think about the most famous statement in the investing world: buy low and sell high. Completely counterintuitive. What this statement is saying, really, is buy when things don't necessarily look great and sell—"

"When they look great," I interrupted. "I've never thought about it, but that's a great point."

"It is hard for people to act in a counterintuitive manner. In fact, they generally act in a very intuitive way."

"It's a lot easier on everyone when all the indicators look great."

"Our relationships with clients tend to become strained when the markets have been difficult. It's particularly tough if this trend continues for a couple of years," Andrew said.

"I guess patience truly is a virtue," I replied.

"The market always rewards patience. The trouble with baby boomers is, we tend to be impatient."

Although Andrew had lumped himself in with the rest of the impatient baby boomers, he showed remarkable patience in lining up his next shot, and I tried to emulate his concentration and focus. We both made it onto the green and sank our putts, then we moved on to the second hole.

"Now, we're early in the round, so this is the perfect time to talk about starting early," Andrew said. We hit our tee shots. Surprisingly, mine landed on the green this time. There's still a little game in these old bones. "Both your investments and your golf game benefit when you have a head start. With investing, it's critical to have enough time to allow interest to compound; with golf, starting young means having time to develop the proper swing mechanics."

"But there are recourses in both golf and investing if you do start late," I said.

"Certainly—in fact, the recourse is the same. You have to work much harder. I know many great golfers who came to the game late. They've had to practise their tails off to get good," Andrew replied. "Now, the key with investing is, you have to be prepared to catch up by contributing a larger percentage of your income than you might have had to if you had started young."

"And that's the tough part—it might be hard to find the money," I said.

"Hard to find the money for investing; hard to find the time for golf," Andrew replied.

We headed off to the third tee. As we hit our tee shots, I noticed something I had missed before: I was using a driver, while Andrew teed off with a three-iron.

"I find this hole to be the toughest on the course," Andrew said. "But what it's taught me is to play within my means. I can't recall ever having a par on this hole. As a result, I've decided to play it as a five instead of a four. I learned this from a couple of older clients who, because of their age, now play every hole one over. I thought it was a brilliant way to manage limitations. I can't reach the green in two strokes, so now I don't even try."

"I've never thought of doing that," I replied.

"It's great—you never try to make a shot you shouldn't. Investors try things they shouldn't all the time. They get in over their heads, and it's just asking for trouble. They, too, need to learn what they are capable of and how to manage their limitations."

Andrew collected the bogey he was trying for, and I made a triple. The old dog was learning something. We headed off to number four.

"This idea is a little complex, so I've saved it for the second par five on this course," Andrew said. "In a nutshell, I believe the average golfer doesn't truly understand the fundamentals of the game. I've played for years, and I've only just begun to understand how to play. Likewise, I believe the average investor doesn't understand the basics of the market."

I let Andrew's words sink in as I walked down the fairway. This could have some interesting implications for the baby boomers. "So, you're saying that, although large numbers of people have become active golfers and investors, they fundamentally don't know what they're doing."

"It's easy to see in golf. Go to a range sometime and watch the myriad of diabolical swings golfers have developed by practising on their own. It's no great surprise that only a small fraction of golfers actually break a hundred. Sadly, it's not just that they're bad—I don't think they know how to improve," Andrew replied.

"And it's the same for investing?"

"It's potentially worse. Many investors now self-direct their accounts, and if the numbers are correct, they are underperforming the market. Most of them just don't know what they need to do to be successful."

"And that would be what, in your opinion?"

"I'm coming to that—all in good time," Andrew replied. I could tell he wanted to keep me guessing for a while.

When we reached the next hole, Andrew continued. "This next idea is relatively simple. Most people don't perform well under pressure. I play with one guy who folds like a tent if you bet a quarter on his next putt. Even pros can fold under pressure. Once they've mastered the game, they have to learn how to play under the intense pressure of tournament golf. Some of the most talented players don't make the big time simply because they can't handle the pressure."

"And many investors have trouble handling the pressure of market fluctuations."

"That's right. They don't obtain the returns they need because the pressure gets to them. The markets are volatile, and many investors get stressed when they see their accounts decline. Golfers need to deal with the pressure of key shots at all levels of play. Similarly, investors need to learn to cope with the stress of volatility, or they will forever struggle in the markets. There's a little book I recommend to my clients called *Golf Is Not a Game of Perfect*, by Dr. Bob Rotella. It's great for the psychology of golf, but it applies to investing and life as well. If you constantly strive for perfection, you'll drive yourself crazy, and you'll never get there anyway. Know the game, know yourself and learn to play to your potential—then relax and enjoy the process."

The sixth hole, perhaps the easiest on the course, was next. It's a short, flat green, really nothing particularly challenging.

"Luck," Andrew said.

"Luck?" I asked.

"Sure. When I think of hitting a hole in one, I think of this hole. I also think of Lee Trevino's famous line that you get luckier the more you practise. You see, pros are more likely to hit a hole in one because they aim at the hole. They know what they're doing, and they practise. Investing is the same: the more you know, the better you are at it. In the end, you make your own luck."

I suddenly remembered a quote I had always liked. "There's a saying I once heard: 'Luck is really no more than preparation meeting opportunity.'"

"That's good. I think I'll use that, if you don't mind," Andrew said.

"So forget luck. Be prepared, stay within your means, and in the end you'll create your own opportunities," I said.

"That's a perfect notion for the markets," Andrew replied.

It was ironic that Andrew had picked this hole to discuss luck. He hit a truly ugly-looking shot that hit the cart path and bounced towards the green. I hit a nice high shot that got caught in the wind and was relegated to the bunker. Luck, I guess.

Seven was up next, another very short hole that was one of the easiest on the course. I found I was anticipating what Andrew would say next.

"I used to step up here and blast away with a driver. It's a short hole, though—you don't need a lot of power." Andrew said.

I walked sheepishly back to my bag and put my driver away.

Andrew continued, "The key is to hit it straight and stay away from the trees on the right. Unless you can hit the ball three hundred yards, there's no reason to take a chance with a driver. Play smart. In the markets, too many people want to go for broke. How many have most of their money in only a few positions? That's what created the tragedies when Nortel went south."

We both put our balls down the middle. I struggled around the green, but we both did okay. We headed off to number eight, a rather long and nasty par three. If I've ever had a par on this hole, I sure don't remember it.

"This is a tough hole. There's just no way around that," Andrew said.

"I know. I always struggle with it."

"And there's no solution to playing this hole other than to improve your game. There's no quick fix."

"I guess we live in an age of quick fixes," I replied, sensing where Andrew was headed.

"If you believe the TV, there's a quick fix for everything," Andrew said. "All you have to do is agree to three easy payments, and the perfect club will solve all your golfing problems. And there are a number of videos and books that claim they can teach you to be a master investor or a skilled day trader. It's just not that easy."

"Both take time, practise and patience."

"The reason golf and investing are so similar is that they look easy but are, in fact, quite difficult and complex. There are no quick fixes for either." Sure enough, Andrew and I both had a tough time with the hole.

On our way to number nine, I realized I was actually playing reasonably well. I hadn't even noticed because I was so fascinated by what Andrew was saying. But I was on the verge of meeting my sub-50 goal and having a chocolate chip muffin.

"I think of this hole as a metaphor for investing or life," Andrew said. "It plays easy if you play it smart. It can also be difficult if you push your luck."

"You have to know when to do certain things and when not to."

"Exactly, and you can develop that ability if you get a coach. A coach can not only improve the way you play golf, but can change the way you approach the course."

"With a few lessons in course management."

"I don't think many people realize the importance of managing the course, as well as themselves. The course doesn't change. Sure, the conditions change, but the course is always fundamentally the same. Some days you shoot well, and some days you don't. A coach can show you both how and what to practise and how to approach the game," Andrew said.

"I've come around to that way of thinking," I replied. "When I started playing several years ago, I just figured, at my age, golf would be a nice bit of exercise. But I've been getting a weekly lesson for a couple of years now. The difference in my game has been significant. I just know more about what I'm trying to do out here. I can't always execute, but at least I know how to try."

"It's the same in the markets. Not only do many investors not seek assistance, but they have a great deal of difficulty recognizing what they're doing wrong. In golf, it becomes obvious when you fire your shot into the woods. With investing, it becomes obvious when your investments get pounded."

"There are lulls in the market and plateaus in your golf game. It's not going to be great all the time. If you're working on a new technique, your game may suffer for a while. But it always gets better if you hang in there."

"And if you do the right things," Andrew said. "That's where coaches are key. They help you stay focused on the end goal."

We finished up on nine, and, miraculously, I achieved my goal: I broke 50. As I munched on a muffin, Andrew explained that he had played golf for years without getting much better. Only when he had a long, hard look at what he wanted from the game was he able to plan a reasonable course of action for improvement. It was then, after some success, that he realized how closely golf relates to investing.

"Okay, number ten," Andrew said, firing an uncharacteristic shot into the trees on the right. "We can draw an analogy between the participants in golf and those in investing."

"Participants?" I asked, not quite understanding where he was going.

"Sure—the average investor is similar to the average golfer. They range in skill level and talent. Some have a keen interest and some a passing interest. The club pro is analogous to an investment advisor, your coach. Then, in golf, you get the touring pros, and even they have a wide range of talent levels and success. In the investing world, these are the pension or portfolio managers. The right combination of players is extremely important, as we saw in the Ryder Cup. The American team lined up a stunning group of world-ranked individuals. But the Europeans, through great teamwork, made short work of the American players. It's a great example of asset mix playing out in the real world. Many of the Europeans grew up with match play golf, and this format favoured their skill set. The Americans, sure of their skill level, assumed they could overpower their opponents, just as many investors believe they can overpower the markets."

Andrew extricated himself from the trees and found the green, and we both putted out for bogeys. The back nine was off to a reasonable start.

As we walked to the next tee, Andrew continued, "Both golf and investing have seen an explosion in mass appeal. It wasn't so long ago that playing golf and investing were exclusively activities of the upper class."

"I guess the changing structure of our society and the economy has led to a surge in many activities once dominated by the rich."

"That's true, but as far as golf and investing are concerned, there's also the cult of personality. Jack Nicklaus was big in his day, but the fame Tiger Woods has is unprecedented. And the investing world now has superstar managers that the media fawn over: Warren Buffett, Peter Lynch, even TV celebrities such as Lou Dobbs."

"Mass media has obviously had a dramatic impact on the development of both activities."

"You're a great straight man for me. That leads right into my next point."

We finished up number eleven. Andrew tapped in for a par, but I wasn't so lucky. Some fool had put a sand trap in a very inconvenient spot. After two tries, I pulled out for a double-bogey.

"Mass media, as you said, has had an enormous impact," Andrew continued. "Fortunes are being made by clever marketers in all aspects of golf and investing. Now the stakes have shot up. For golf, that's great. Players make more, golf companies make more, advertisers can leverage off it. However, higher stakes and higher volatility may not be good for investors. It's great that Mike Weir sunk a putt for a million dollars at the Masters. Including endorsements and future opportunities, it was worth a whole lot more than that. But some pros don't thrive as the stakes go up, and I think that's the case for many investors."

"So, as media attention has caused the markets to become more active, investors have started to struggle."

"I think that's true for a large number of people."

"And the solution?" I asked, with my best "you brought it up" look.

"Next hole," Andrew replied, laughing.

We moved to the thirteenth tee, and Andrew sat down on a bench. "There's no one around. Why don't we take a break?" he said. I joined him, and he continued. "This one's a little theoretical, but bear with me for a moment. Imagine for a second that you've made it into the club championship match, and you're going to play the best golfer in the club."

"That would be *very* theoretical," I said with a laugh, "but go on."

"Let's say there was a little-known rule that said someone could play for you, the club pro, perhaps."

I thought for a moment. "No, if I had made it to that point, I think I would want to play it myself."

"I think that's likely," Andrew replied. "But imagine the pro agreed to carry your bag and advise you on every shot and on course management. Wouldn't that be a big plus? Well, think about investing. You *can* get someone to play for you. You might want to do it yourself, but think how much better off you'd be if someone was making the 'investment shots' for you." Andrew rose and walked over to the tee. I pried myself up from the bench and followed.

For the rest of the hole, neither of us spoke. I was thinking hard about what Andrew had just said.

Andrew broke our silence only when we arrived at fourteen, a very short par five. "My thought for this hole is: don't let your last shot affect your next one. It's over; let it go. If you've made a bad shot, don't get upset about it and let your focus slip, or you will miss your next shot too. If you've made a great shot, don't get cocky, as over-confidence can also cause you to make mistakes. This lesson carries over into investing, and into life, for that matter. We shouldn't dwell on the past, but we *should* learn from it; try to understand what went wrong—or right."

"There's always something to learn from both successes and mistakes," I said.

"Exactly. All is not lost just because you've made a mistake—especially if you learn from it. Here's a case in point: Vijay Singh, who recently won the Canadian Open, triple-bogeyed the same hole twice over the first three days. On the last day, he parred it. Obviously, he had learned something from his early mistakes—and despite those mistakes, he still managed to win the tournament!"

We putted out, and Andrew had his first birdie of the

day. I wasn't as fortunate: another poorly placed bunker and another double-bogey.

Fifteen is a tough hole. We hit our tee shots and walked over to the canteen for water.

"As we play these last few holes, here's a quick thought you might want to consider. I find, even in my relatively youthful mid-forties, that I can start to lose my focus on these last couple of holes," Andrew said.

"At my age, it's fatigue," I replied.

"Well, either way, it's a good analogy for investing. You have to stay focused on every shot, on every hole, right to the end. Investments require our attention all the way through. That's one reason almost everyone needs assistance: other activities in their lives make it impossible for them to give enough attention to their investments. It's impossible to stay on top of everything all the time, unless you have help."

We moved to our second shots, over a ravine that always acts like a ball magnet for me. This time, with some kind of divine intervention, I made it over the valley of doom and stayed out of trouble.

"That was a good shot," Andrew said. "Even though you started late, I can tell you have a good temperament for the game."

"At my age, there's no point in getting overly excited," I responded.

"I agree. Really, there's no point in getting overly excited at any age. But I've seen many players just lose it out here. I used to get very upset when I was younger. Because I wasn't playing often, my game declined, and it became very frustrating. I eventually gave it up for several years when my children were young. I didn't have the time or the temperament to play at the level I wanted to play at."

"I imagine you're going to relate this to investing too. Am I right?"

"Good call," Andrew said. "Some people shouldn't be in the markets. They don't have the temperament. If you can't handle the precise nature of golf, go play tennis. If you can't handle watching the markets ebb and flow—and many can't—put your money into a savings account. Golf is a great game, and the enjoyment of it, I believe, goes up as you get older. Investing is also great, and the rewards can be significant. But we need to truly assess whether these activities are for us."

We finished up and headed to number sixteen, my favourite hole on the course. Standing on the tee, you get a beautiful view of the clubhouse. I often linger here for a few minutes; it's on this hole that I remember why I like the game so much.

As I was taking in the scenery, Andrew continued with his next idea, "This is the best driving hole on the course. It's like teeing up a ball at the end of a wharf and trying to hit the ocean."

"It's easily my favourite hole," I responded. "But it's the view that has me hooked."

"Okay, here's a pop quiz: what's the most important aspect of golf?"

"I know this—it's the putting." I felt quite smug in my knowledge of the game.

"A hole like this can make you forget that, because it's such a great driving hole," Andrew said. "You want to get up and just rip it. Most guys can't help themselves; it's almost a compulsion. But up ahead are two very tough bunkers and a pretty fast green. It's the short game that makes or breaks this hole—and golf in general. It's no different for pro golfers. You'll notice that the great hitters are often nowhere near the top of the money list, even though they have an advantage in getting to the green quickly. It's the leading putters who are almost always at the top. For hackers like us, the short game is important, but staying out of trouble—those nasty bunkers—is key."

"And most of us forget that when we're at the tee," I replied. At least Andrew had included himself in the hacker category.

"How many people talk up their putting or chipping abilities? Not many. But they sure do go on and on about the drive they ripped last week."

"And the similarity with investing is what?" I asked.

"Well, most people believe stock selection is the be-all and end-all. Picking winners, outsmarting everyone else. In fact, study after study has shown that stock selection accounts for next to nothing. The real key is proper asset mix," Andrew replied.

"So, we need to know what activities are crucial, focus our attention there, and try to stay out of trouble," I concluded.

After all that, both of us landed in the same bunker. Andrew was able to extricate himself for a bogey. I wasn't quite as lucky. I seemed to be making a habit of double-bogeys.

We walked over to the seventeenth tee. "This is a hard hole to screw up," Andrew said, lining up his tee shot.

"Oh, I've found a few ways to do it," I responded.

"We all have at some time. What we have to remember is that golf is a very difficult game with a tiny margin of error. I believe golf is one of the hardest games to play. You're hitting a tiny ball with a club that has a very small hitting surface."

"And the ball doesn't move."

"Exactly. Unlike hockey or baseball or tennis, the ball just sits there. You have as much time to think about it as you need."

"Plenty of time to drive yourself crazy."

"That's why the game is so psychologically challenging. Even pros mess up, and you can watch the pressure eating away at them. I'm certain it's the toughest game to make a living at," Andrew said.

"We just see the cream of the crop who've made it. We don't see the ones who flamed out under pressure."

"And the market's a tough game too," Andrew said. "There's often a very small margin of error. Like golf, the market sits in front of us, waiting for us to react. To make our shot, so to speak. And it gives us a great deal of time between shots to think about what we are doing. But if we mis-hit in the market, the consequences can be dramatic. Sports like hockey and tennis, on the other hand, are more like owning a home: you just go with the flow of the play."

We putted out and headed for the last hole. I wondered what idea Andrew would finish up with.

"If we're fortunate, we can continue to play golf well into our senior years. Heck, I'd even suggest that it's a great way to stay in shape as we age," Andrew said.

"Playing golf has so many benefits as we age, and the exercise is just part of it. Because of the golf handicapping system, we can continue to compete on a level playing field. No other game offers that. Golf gets us out of the house, gives us something to do, which can be critical as we age. It allows us to create a social network, something that is especially important for men in retirement—we're not as good as women at maintaining social contacts. And camaraderie is important because it helps us exercise our minds."

"We also need to keep investing as we get older. These days, we can't become too conservative and just go to cash—we run the risk of running out of money if we live long enough. We need to adjust our asset mix to our changing realities, just as we adjust our golf game to our changing physical abilities. But we should never, ever give up trying,"

"That's why I'm out here trying to shoot my age," I said. "I'll keep trying until I can't lift a club. I figure my best chance will come in about fifteen years."

Andrew looked a bit dubious, given the way I play. But we all need to have goals.

We finished up the eighteenth. Andrew shot an 84, and I broke 100 for the first time in over a year. It was probably because I wasn't thinking about my game at all.

We had a quick lemonade on the deck, and Andrew handed me a list of ten common principles of investing and golf. "I shortened it to ten—it's the Letterman effect. These are the things we need to focus on if we want to be a success. Use them in your book if they help."

With that, Andrew headed off to the showers and back to work. I sat on the porch for a few minutes and reviewed the list.

GOLF

1. Is it repeatable?
2. Play what you're given.
3. Get a coach.
4. There are no quick fixes.
5. Play within your means.
6. Know the game.
7. Play the percentages.
8. Know what you want from the game.
9. Work to improve or quit.
10. Practise, practise, practise.

INVESTING

1. Do you have a process?
2. Respond to the realities of the markets.
3. Seek advice.
4. Have a long-term view.
5. Understand your risk tolerance.
6. Know yourself.
7. Create a manageable asset mix.
8. Know your goals.
9. Manage the markets or buy a GIC.
10. Diversity, diversify, diversify.

14
Freedom Seventy-five

HAZEN

In the fall, it's almost as if a small toggle switch gets flipped in the back of our brains and our mindsets change. Those long, sultry summer days give us a chance to relax and slow down for a while. Then, wham, September rolls around, and we're called once again into action. I think it's stuck way back in the recesses of our subconscious, that childhood "back to school" training we received when we were young. Years later, that training kicks us into high gear in the fall as our vocational call to arms.

Ruth and I needed to get down to work on our much-anticipated book project. We had slacked off for the summer, and it felt great. Ruth certainly needed the break after her years of routine in academia. I thought it would be good for her to at least retire for the summer. We had kicked off our long-discussed tour of Europe with a two-week visit to Naples and Venice. We wanted to see how our theories about aging are playing out in a country that will face pension and health care issues years ahead of us. The Italians have a novel solution to worries about the future: relax. There's something to be learned from them, but it's a tough lesson for Canadians. We've worked hard as a country to earn our reputation as worriers, so I guess we should damn well be proud of it.

We hadn't completely taken the summer off. Ruth had had some very interesting discussions with Meredith, and I'd had a wonderful time talking to Andrew Proctor about the financial issues our aging population faces. The research for our book was never very far from our thoughts. Summer had been a time to slowly gather our ideas. I believe all good ideas are like a good cup of tea: you have to let them steep for a while. When they're ready, you'll know.

The timing of our project couldn't be better. The issues our country is facing today are significant, and many of them are the consequence of an unusual population distribution. Canada produced 480,000 babies in 1959, a record that still stands today. That's approximately double the number of babies born in 1939. What that means is that the number of Canadians over age sixty-five will double over the next twenty years. Because we have also suffered a precipitous drop in our birth rate since the mid-sixties, the number of Canadian seniors as a percentage of the population is set to explode. There is a growing risk for Canadians who don't prepare for these trends. There will be obvious pressures on both health care and pensions. Governments generally prepare for the next election, not for issues citizens will face years from now.

Ruth and I have always had some disagreement on what issues are most important to an aging society. Given her work, she is concerned about our collective social and emotional well-being. I am more concerned about whether the boomers will have enough loot. But these issues may be two sides of the same coin. They say money doesn't buy happiness, but it doesn't buy sadness either. As a generation, the boomers are going to have to work on their collective well-being as they approach retirement. And they need to consider what that costs.

These were our thoughts as we headed into the first few weeks of fall.

Meredith was set to join us in a few days so we could arrange our research schedule and decide on the rules of engagement during our great debate. After some initial discussion over breakfast, we decided we would each continue researching our particular areas of interest. We could then pull it all together and see where the lifestyle issues met the financial ones.

We headed out to our new and improved garden and slid into a couple of Muskoka chairs to throw around some of our ideas. "Let me start off with an idea from Canada's leading futurist, Richard Worzel," I said, holding up his book *Facing the Future*. "He suggests we're much better off if we anticipate what the future holds, rather than relying on the traditional forecasting that economists place such stock in. Forecasts, which attempt to give an accurate view of the future, tend to be wrong much of the time. They try to be too precise, which isn't what we need. A general sense of what might happen is much more useful as we try to position ourselves for the financial and emotional challenges that lie ahead. Anticipating helps us better understand what will affect future events and allows us to prepare with the appropriate actions."

"That takes us back to the David Foot versus Michael Adams debate," Ruth replied. "Demographics tell us how many Canadians there are at different stages of life. They may not, however, tell us what those Canadians are thinking or doing. We can better anticipate what they might do if we look at what they've already done."

"We're working well together already," I said, and we both started to laugh.

"So the biggest issue for our largest generation has to be their pending retirement," Ruth continued.

"It's pending, but it's still a ways off. And the boomers' struggle to be ready for retirement continues to be not only an enormous social issue, but also an economic issue," I responded.

"What a shock it must be for the baby boomers to discover, as they close in on age fifty-five, that they are nowhere near ready to retire—either economically or emotionally," Ruth said, pulling out some notes.

"I read an interesting article on retirement the other day that casually mentioned 'freedom seventy-five.' It caught my eye because I've heard a number of people use that expression over the past few years," I said.

"Individuals need to think about when retirement is appropriate, both for themselves and for the country as a whole," Ruth said. "Economically, we can't afford to have the boomers retire early; we're going to need them in the workforce. The government is going to need to rethink some of its policies to keep these folks working. Fortunately, the retirement age is starting to be pushed back." I knew retirement issues had been a significant part of her academic work, and she was showing the same passion discussing it now.

"There's something that has always puzzled me about the notion of early retirement," I said. "If the average person starts full-time work at, let's say, twenty-five, then they'll work for thirty years before they hit their mid-fifties. It may take them twenty years to hit their stride in their profession, so they have ten years—if they're lucky—of peak earning."

"I think I see where you're going with this. The numbers don't add up," Ruth replied.

"No, because they're likely to live for almost thirty years after that. Plus, during those thirty years of working full-time, they have to pay off a house, raise their children, maybe go on a trip every now and then, and still somehow save enough to be in retirement for thirty years," I responded.

"I think we should turn the idea of Freedom 55 on its head and think of it as the freedom to *work* until you're seventy-five. That would reflect what many Canadians are already doing. The boomers identify with their work, they enjoy it—they want to keep working. I think we need to empower them by telling them that not only is it okay to keep going on your own terms, but the economy needs you to do so." As Ruth spoke, she was writing feverishly. Bouncing ideas off each other was going to be very useful for us. We always have, but not like this—with a specific purpose in mind.

After a moment, she looked up. "Older people also need to stay active. Even if you *can* retire, it's not necessarily a good idea to go ahead and do so. In days gone by, people wanted to retire because work was very physical. Today, our economy has advanced rapidly, and most jobs are suitable for mature workers."

"Look at me," I replied. "Work keeps you young. It keeps your mind in shape. It also allows us to stay connected with others. This is especially important for older men, who don't have as many social connections outside the workplace as women do."

Ruth pulled from her research file a recent study from the American Association of Retired People. It turns out that 80 percent of boomers want to continue to work into retirement in some form or another, 30 percent working part-time for enjoyment, 25 percent working part-time for income, 15 percent starting a business, 7 percent working full-time in a new career and 3 percent doing some other type of work.

"So much for early retirement," I said. "It comes as no great shock that boomers are changing the landscape, and it's good news that they want to work, because a recent Statistics Canada report noted that seniors are the only large pool of untapped labour."

"Okay, let's keep moving along. Here's the next big issue we need to tackle," Ruth said, handing me a couple of articles.

The first was about the changing nature of our society. The second was about social capital. This was an issue Ruth and I had bandied about over the years: what is Canada's social structure going to look and feel like in the coming years? Obviously, on average, we're an aging population. But how will this trend play out?

"Personally, I feel rather upbeat about our society's future," Ruth said.

"Well, I always feel that way," I said, "but I'm interested to hear your reasoning."

"I think much of the negative sentiment about society ignores the shift we're seeing in our population. Here's a great example." Ruth handed me Robert Putnam's classic

Bowling Alone. "Professor Putnam is deeply concerned about the growing disconnectedness in our society. Participation in social groups—be they political parties, citizens' organizations, religious groups or even informal social gatherings—has been in decline over the past twenty to thirty years. But I think what Putnam sees as growing alienation may have more to do with the time of life the boomers find themselves in. As we become older, a large part of our population is entering their busiest years. The boomers are at the most demanding time in their careers. Their children still make demands on their time, and a growing number have to deal with the declining health of their parents. They are being pulled in many directions, and society is suffering as a result. But eventually—it's inevitable—their children will become productive adults. And, unfortunately, their parents will pass away. The boomers will get their time back, and I suspect we will see an enormous resurgence of social capital."

"Here's what's interesting to me," I said. "Dr. Reginald Bibby, one of Canada's leading sociologists, has a different take from Putnam, at least as far as religious groups are concerned. The dean of 'what Canada's thinking' has uncovered what he believes to be a renewed interest in organized religion in this country. In his recent book *Restless Gods: The Renaissance of Religion in Canada*, he confirms that faith has a significant place in our lives. It's no great shock, given their independent nature, that the baby boomers went on a search for something new when they were younger. They are well educated, and smart people challenge institutions and ask questions. But it turns out that the baby boomers never lost the need for spirituality.

Many have found something new that works for them, but some have found comfort back where they began. Their renewed faith makes sense in an aging population. As we get a little older, we want to believe there is something else beyond this life."

"The key words are 'a little' older," Ruth replied. "The media still aren't sure how to characterize the boomers. I have often heard them called the 'retiring generation.' And that couldn't be further from the truth."

"That reminds me of something else I want to work into our book. I believe the boomers are younger than their parents were at the same age." I paused to let Ruth think about that idea for a moment. "*We've* certainly always thought of ourselves as ten years younger than we really are, but the baby boomers are pushing that notion even further."

"Because they are living longer, they're pushing back all the usual age thresholds," Ruth responded.

"Exactly. Do you know what the average age for marriage is now?"

"As it happens, I do. I was just talking to Meredith about that very thing the other day. Men thirty-four, women thirty-two."

"You amaze me: you have a mind like a steel trap when it comes to remembering statistics. You're right, of course. And because of this, women are reproducing later—no wonder our birth rate is down. If everyone reproduces in their thirties, there will only be three generations per century, as opposed to the four we have had in the past."

"And people buy big homes in their fifties because they're planning to hang around for another forty years. That may explain the changing trends in real estate you've been discussing with Andrew. I'm convinced; let's put that idea on the list." Ruth stood up for a stretch just as Dylan came wandering through the back gate. Ruth had neglected to tell me he was dropping by for lunch.

"This is a nice life, hanging out in the garden. I wish my life were this relaxed," Dylan said, joining us.

"Be careful what you wish for," I said.

"Actually," Ruth added. "Your father and I are jotting down ideas we want to include in our book." We got up and started into the kitchen.

"I've given your great literary endeavour some thought," Dylan replied. "And I have some ideas you may want to include."

"Your generation has good ideas?" I asked, getting the look of disdain I was hoping for.

"Yeah, every now and then we have an inspiration or two," Dylan said dryly.

Ruth was busily pulling things out of the fridge. "I made your favourite, Dylan: lemon linguine casserole. In exchange, we're expecting at least a couple of good ideas."

We sat down at the kitchen table. "One of the things universities are very serious about these days is ethics," Dylan said. "They feel they didn't spend enough time on ethics in the past, and they are making up for it in spades. Because I did a joint MBA and law degree, I spent an enormous amount of time learning about ethics."

"And you think we should devote a section of our book to this topic?" Ruth asked.

"You can't legislate or force people to act ethically," Dylan replied. "What they need to understand is that unethical behaviour directly hurts them and also harms society in general. Look at the people at Enron or WorldCom—what was the result of their bad behaviour? All of them will do prison time, but the real damage is to the public's confidence in public companies. And look at Martha Stewart—she even had a second chance to come clean, and she still couldn't manage to understand that she had a responsibility, both to herself and to the millions of people watching her, to act ethically."

"So we need to reinforce the idea that ethical behaviour, both personally and in business, is a win-win proposition," I responded.

"The baby boomers, in particular, seem to need a reminder," Dylan said. "They started out with very lofty ideals. But many of these same people are at the centre of corporate scandals."

"And what's your academic take on that?" I asked.

Dylan paused for a moment to wolf down an unusually large forkful of linguine. "Boomers were susceptible to greed, just like everyone else, despite their youthful idealism. In one of my courses, we reviewed corporate scandals throughout history. It turns out that corporate scandals are always seen during boom times. In the end, all you can do is put regulations in place and make sure that enforcement acts as a deterrent. But the schools feel they can have a positive impact on future generations if they spend time showing that ethics pay."

"Do you feel the focus on ethics was effective?" Ruth asked.

"They certainly made us aware of ethical issues, which I think is important," Dylan replied. "When opportunities present themselves, and they will, we know we have a responsibility to think through what we're doing. Many universities also make students sign a letter of integrity before they can graduate. Schools believe their graduates are representing them in the business world, and they want that to always be a positive."

"That's really terrific. I didn't know they did that," I said. It was confirmed: Ruth and I got our money's worth on Dylan's education.

"There's a second issue I think you must address, and this one concerns everyone in North America, not just your favourite generation," Dylan continued.

I knew where he was headed; we had spoken of this issue a great deal over the past couple of years.

"Security is going to continue to be a major concern. I think September 11 will prove to be a watershed event," Dylan said.

"Everyone is suddenly feeling more vulnerable," Ruth suggested.

"That's part of it," Dylan replied. "We've felt awfully secure since the fall of the Berlin Wall. We need to look back well over a hundred years to find any serious acts of war on North American soil. Pearl Harbor was an exception, but Hawaii is a long way from continental America. Let's face it, we were feeling extremely insulated, and that came crashing down with the Twin Towers."

"Part of the problem is the media as well," I said. "You know they are going to feed on the public's fear and make the situation much worse."

"I've looked at some polling data," Ruth added, "The sense of insecurity is going to be a big issue for businesses and politicians alike. During the Cold War, we saw the sides line up along political and ideological lines. It was only a matter of time before the communist system cracked. But this time we're dealing with cultural and religious issues, and the dispute will likely be tougher to resolve."

"I've looked at those data as well," I said. "Because of our wealth and education levels, we are much more tuned in to world events, and there is a strong sense that we've got a lot to lose. I believe we will be calling on our government more and more to provide security, and less and less to play its traditional role of benevolent overseer. North Americans are feeling very confident—we've done well, and we've created a powerful economic system—and yet we're also feeling vulnerable. We'll look to our governments to protect us. Wealth isn't much use if you can't enjoy reasonable levels of security."

"This is awfully serious stuff to be discussing over lunch," Dylan broke in, trying to lighten the mood.

"You started it," Ruth laughed.

"Remember the Boy Scout motto," I said. "Be prepared. That's what we're trying to accomplish with this book. We want it to be a heads-up to those planning for the future. Have a sense of what could crop up, but also be prepared to respond to the unexpected."

"On that note, I have to prepare to depart—I have a meeting at two," Dylan said, inhaling the last morsels on his plate. "But before I skedaddle, there is one other idea I wanted to mention.

"Okay, fire away," I replied.

"I think you should include a piece in your book on gratitude," Dylan continued. "The boomers have done enormously well, better economically than any other generation. I think it would be useful for them, as they age, to acknowledge their fortune and seek ways to share it."

"I've thought about that a great deal. I suspect that as the boomers hit fifty they will come around to your way of thinking," Ruth replied. "But it certainly wouldn't hurt to prod them a little."

"I hate to drop deep intellectual notions and run," Dylan said, "but I've got to get going."

Dylan kissed his mother, gave me a jaunty salute and ran out the door. His input had given Ruth and me even more to think about.

15
Tacticians versus Strategists

HAZEN

We had finished our first week of heavy lifting on our research into the issues we face as an aging nation. Meredith had joined us on Monday and quickly brought an interesting perspective to our project. She's not just researching these issues; she gets to live them.

The baby boomers, who didn't trust anyone over thirty, now find fifty sneaking up on them. Turning fifty will never be the same again. It used to be a time of slowing down and preparing for retirement. It has now become a time of renewal. In *Age Power*, America's guru on aging, Dr. Ken Dychtwald, coined the word "middlescence" to describe those aged forty to sixty. Like adolescence, middlescence is a time of personal growth and reinvention. The boomers aren't slowing down, they're just shifting gears. Their children are leaving the nest, and the second half of their lives is unfolding before them. We'll all have to hold on to our hats as they change everything in this country.

For the next several months, Ruth, Meredith and I will be occupied with research reports, polling data, institutional studies and Statistics Canada analyses, but not tonight. Every three months, I'm charged $400 by the golf course for food and beverages, whether I use it or not. During the summer, it is usually pretty easy to use up the minimum. This summer, however, had been a little unusual. I'd played a reasonable number of games, but Ruth and I hadn't had much of a chance to eat out at the club restaurant. The weather has been cool, and we've been busy. So tonight Ruth and I were treating the DeMarcos to dinner. The forecast looked great, and there's nothing like a mild fall evening spent watching a few groups finish their rounds while you enjoy drinks and a nice dinner.

We were set to pick Pieter and Meredith up at 6:30 so we'd be at the club before it got dark. When we pulled up to their house, they were sitting in wrought-iron chairs by the front door.

"Hop aboard, folks," I said.

"It's awfully nice of you to take us to dinner," Pieter said as he and Meredith got into the back seat.

"Not to mention the personal limo service," Meredith added.

"As I told you at the house today, Meredith, use it or lose it," I responded. "We normally have our quarterly fee used up by now, but this has been a different kind of summer. Anyway, it's a great chance for us to catch up."

We chatted the whole way to the club. Pieter wanted to hear about our trip to Italy. It was one of the places he and Meredith had put on their travel wish list. When we pulled up, the parking lot looked reasonably clear. It gets a whole lot less busy at this time of year. We wandered in and got a great table up front with a perfect view of the last hole.

"Okay, let's have some fun." I reached into my pocket and pulled out a handful of loonies. Pieter and Meredith looked perplexed, but Ruth knew exactly what was going on.

"He really is still a kid," she said, shaking her head. But even as she said this, she pulled some loonies from her purse. She, too, can be a kid.

"Here's how the game works," I said. "As the next foursome comes over the hill, we all pick a player. If your player pots the ball first, you win the loonie for that hole. We should be able to watch five or six groups before it gets dark."

Pieter and Meredith each pulled out some change. "What happens if someone putts out of order?" Pieter asked.

I smiled. "That's the beauty of the game. The person you pick could have a one-foot tap in, but if he picks up his ball, you lose. Someone could putt out of turn, but if it's the first in, you win. Keeps it interesting."

"We can talk at the same time," Ruth said, giving me the "we didn't come here to bet on strangers" look.

"Okay, here's the first group," I said, as a foursome came over the hill two hundred yards out. "You two get to pick first."

"I'll take the guy in red," Meredith said, plunking down her loonie.

"I'll take the guy with the pull cart," Pieter said.

Ruth and I each took a player, and we settled in and ordered drinks. This was a good chance for us to catch up, with Pieter especially—I hadn't seen much of him since our dinner at their place in late May.

"How was your summer?" I asked him as our drinks arrived.

"It was a time of adjustment and change for us," Pieter responded. "Malcolm was away all summer, and Emily was busy with her job at the Body Shop. Meredith and I are trying to prepare for life on our own again."

"Don't think empty nest just yet," Ruth said. "Children have a funny habit of coming back to the roost after college these days." We all had a good laugh.

"Okay, here's where the golf gets interesting," I said. All the players had successfully coaxed their balls onto the green. Pieter's player rimmed his putt and then casually picked it up and put it in his pocket. Meredith grabbed the hole when her player tapped in. "I like this game," she said, gathering up her winnings.

"You see? It's a great game," I said, looking over at Pieter.

The next group—a threesome—came into view. "So what do we do when there are only three players?" Pieter asked.

"Meredith has to sit out, because she won the last hole," I replied.

"Now, where were we?" Ruth asked. "Oh, yes, empty nests. Many children are remaining at home longer these days. And more and more baby boomers are providing homes for their aging parents. Boomers have to deal with demands from above and below. They're certainly going to have a lot on their plates over the next several years."

We took a few minutes to order dinner and watch the next group putt out. I had it in the bag until my player was conceded a four-footer, which certainly pushed the outer limits of what could be called a gimme. The problem with this game is, you can't charge onto the green when you've been wronged. You pay your loonie and take your chances. Ruth's player got close, and then tapped in for the victory. She makes fun of me, but she likes this game—and she likes it even better when she wins.

"The other big thing for us this summer, of course, was sorting out our financial plan and our life plan," Meredith said. "Pieter and I hit that critical point when we have to know where we're going. Jamie certainly helped us understand the importance of having a plan."

"A plan is fundamental," I said. "It's really quite astounding that so many investors wade into the markets without some basic guidelines to govern their actions."

"What really struck me was the importance of a written document. You not only have to go to the trouble of gathering the data, you need to have a written covenant to keep both parties accountable and focused," Meredith replied.

"One thing I keep thinking about is Jamie's observation that the recent correction in the market came late," Pieter said. "Because the boomers infused such momentum into the markets in the nineties, the cycle ran on longer than usual. The result was a larger correction and more damage than was necessary."

"Many investors were getting away with poor form in the markets, so they just kept doing what they were doing," I responded. "In fact, as the markets took off, especially on the tech side, investors wanted to ramp up their exposure."

"Then the correction came. Now let's hope they are searching out the proper way to go about their business," Meredith said.

"I hope that's what the boomers, at least, are doing," I replied. "Andrew feels that the markets will be in good shape if your generation can learn proper management techniques over the next decade. But if they continue to approach the market in a fly-by-the-seat-of-your-pants kind of way, they are in for a rough ride as they get older."

"And how optimistic was he?" Ruth asked.

"Actually, he was very optimistic. All the major banks and investment firms are prioritizing planning with clients. He was encouraged that the importance of planning was sinking in," I said. "And financial advisors have been aided in this process by some terrific software."

We paused for a moment when the appetizers arrived. The next group was now on the green. My player, for some odd reason, picked up her ball. Meredith's player got close on his putt, and one of the other players knocked it in for him. In this game, everything counts. Meredith was definitely enjoying herself. We turned our focus back to the salads and our conversation.

"Learning how to execute the plan after you've set it up was probably the most important piece for me, because it's where I've struggled the most," Pieter said. "Jamie boiled it down to two simple choices: you're either a strategist or a tactician."

"I had a similar discussion with Andrew out here on the golf course," I said.

"I'm sorry. Can you explain the difference between tactical and strategic in this context?" Ruth asked.

"Sure," Pieter replied. "A tactician tries to play the market like a game of chess. As each move takes place, you need to think about it and make your countermove reasonably quickly."

"And in strategic thinking you have a long-term plan, and you stick with it," I said. "You make a move only at regular intervals, quarterly perhaps, and only to put your plan back on track."

"What I've learned this summer is that a huge majority of boomers have tried to act like tacticians. I was one of them. We want to self-direct and do battle with the investment markets. Unfortunately, the outcome for many of us wasn't what it could have been," Pieter said.

"I think the reason that Andrew is optimistic is that there are some promising trends developing," I said. "The investment firms have a better understanding of the challenges of human nature and are encouraging investors to be more strategic in their approach to investing. The mainstream acceptance of a planning process also allows them to bring consistency and accountability to bear. Something our boomers can always use."

"That's a perfect lead-in for a very cerebral idea that's been rolling around in my head for a couple of weeks," Meredith said. "I think we need to include it in the book."

"You've got our attention," I said.

"Bear with me: it's still an intellectual work-in-progress," Meredith continued. "I was intrigued by Gregg Easterbrook's argument in *The Progress Paradox* that many of our decisions and actions are influenced by our DNA. We are hardwired to be anxious or fearful, and because we are descended from hunter-gatherers, we hoard things."

"I agree—it was very interesting," Ruth replied.

"Maybe we need to cross disciplines and consider psychology. In Psych 101, you learn the notion of fight or flight. It's an instinctive survival technique. Jamie and

Andrew say investors need to have a plan so they don't react to anxiety. The problem is, we may be predisposed to react. When something goes wrong, we want to fight—invest in something else—or flee and go to cash. It's not in our nature to sit and do nothing."

"That's intriguing, Meredith," Hazen broke in. "You're right: we need to think more about the impact of psychology on our behaviour in the markets."

"It affects our personal lives as well," Meredith replied. "As the Eagles sang in "Learn to Be Still," we need to learn to relax and smell the roses. But that might be difficult because of the instincts simmering below the surface."

"We haven't come as far as we think," Ruth said. "That's a great idea, Meredith. We'll certainly want to develop it. I know just the person to call at the university."

Dusk was slowly closing in, but we had one last group to watch. My player hit a beautiful clip to two feet, the kiss of death for this game. He walked up and marked his ball. Ruth's player four-putted, but managed to be the first in. It was a clean sweep for the women tonight, which they celebrated by high-fiving across the table. And Ruth makes fun of my adolescent streak!

Dinner arrived, a surf and turf delight of steak and salmon. I'd ordered an Australian Chardonnay to go with it. Ruth valiantly offered to abstain and get our group home safely. Our conversation rolled on.

"I have to say, this summer I've learned a lot about the realities of investing, and the realities don't necessarily align with the theories I've had over the years." I paused for a moment. "On that note, I have an apology of sorts to offer you."

I had caught Pieter and Meredith off guard. "Why would you need to apologize, Hazen? You've always been wonderful to us!" Meredith said.

"When I encouraged you to start investing, I thought everything would look after itself. But when we played golf back in May, Pieter, it became apparent that your experience with the markets had turned out to be less than optimal."

"But that's not your fault," Pieter replied.

"I know, but I felt responsible. The investment markets have turned out to be a unique challenge for you boomers. The only solution is process, process, process."

"That's what Jamie and Andrew say. The markets are tougher than we think—certainly emotionally—so we have to lay out a strategic course of action and stick to it," Pieter said.

"Are they opposed to a tactical approach to investing, then?" Ruth asked.

"No, I wouldn't say that," Pieter replied. "Andrew, in particular, believes the tactical approach will work as long as you take responsibility for what you're doing. You need to be plugged in to the markets, and you need to respond to the advice you're given. He feels, however, that there are very few people who are capable of this."

"The trouble is, the media encourage boomers to be tacticians with the stories they publish," Meredith said. "One of Canada's leading magazines ran a cover story last year: 'The Complete Guide to Retirement Investing.' They do it every year. A few chosen gurus pick the hot mutual fund sectors. That's not a guide—it's hype. It's articles like that one that confused me and made me feel flustered. After this summer, though, I finally feel I'm beginning to understand what we need to do and, better yet, how to do it."

"To my mind, the most important point is one Pieter brought up a moment ago, and that's taking responsibility," Ruth said. "The greatest lesson we can learn is that we are the ones who are ultimately responsible for our health, our finances, our lives. A good part of our book is going to be an analysis of what burdens the boomers these days. I believe that, to some degree, they are still victims of recent history."

Ruth had been unusually quiet during dinner, but she certainly had our attention now.

"I thought you believed the boomers had fared pretty well so far," Meredith said.

"I do," Ruth responded, "but look at the events of the last seventy-five years, events that shaped who their parents are and thus who they are: the Depression confirmed that life is tough. As a result, we got unprecedented public spending and social reform, followed by an enormous ramp-up in the economy due to wartime industrialization."

"After the war, this economy served as an engine to supply the world. We also had a much more highly skilled labour force," I added.

"When our soldiers came back from the war, Canada owed them a great debt. As a result, education rates shot up and the start of universal home ownership took off. But the real key to who the baby boomers are is that the generation that lived through the Depression wanted something better for their children." Ruth took a sip of water.

"So their children—the boomers—grew up in a completely different environment," Meredith commented.

"Exactly. As you know from your work, Meredith, members of a generation are influenced by the common experiences they've had growing up. The boomer generation has had a great run economically and, as a result, may suffer from greater expectations," Ruth replied.

"That's true, Ruth," Pieter said. "I think we're in a hurry. I think we want a lot, and I think we struggle with what's truly important."

"And *I* think that's the great challenge as you boomers head out for the second half," I replied. "Can you filter what you've learned and apply it? You need to, because the stakes get higher as you get older."

"That's where the plan will come into play for me," Pieter said. "As you say, the stakes are high—I can't get off track as I've done in the past."

We were quiet for a moment, concentrating on our food. As I was thinking about Pieter's last comment, I remembered something I wanted to mention to him. "I read a book over the summer, Pieter, that I think you'll find useful. It's called *Good to Great*. The author, Jim Collins, is a professor at Stanford University in California. I think it may help you with a number of things. You should read it too, Meredith."

"What's it about?" Meredith asked.

"Well, the purpose of the book is to define why some companies go on to greatness and some don't. But I think there's a message there that all of us can use."

"I've read it as well," Ruth chimed in. "It really is a good book."

"The great companies confronted their problems and took action," I continued. "They then put the right people in place to help them achieve their goals. I think that's what you've been trying to do this summer."

"I'd love to borrow the book, if you're offering," Pieter replied.

"Sure, Pieter. There's another idea in there you might want to consider," I went on. "The author refers to something he calls the 'Stockdale paradox.' Admiral Jim Stockdale was a prisoner of war during the Vietnam War. The author asked him which of the POWs made it home, and Admiral Stockdale said the realists. They were able to confront the brutal reality of their situation and get through it. The optimists thought they'd be home by Christmas, then Easter—and then Christmas would come around again. Slowly, they lost their will to live."

"Viktor Frankl lived through a similar experience in the death camps of the Second World War," Ruth said. "But he felt the key to survival was having a vision of the future, the idea that your work is not done. He's the one who recommended that the U.S. put up a Statue of Responsibility on the west coast to match the Statue of Liberty in the east."

"That's a great message for the boomers when they're stressed or feel they aren't getting a fair shake," Meredith said.

"If you haven't experienced adversity, it's tough to keep things in context," Ruth replied.

"Another good book for the boomers might be John Steinbeck's *The Grapes of Wrath*," I said. "We've come a long way in a few generations, and we need to remember that."

"We need to remind ourselves that, whatever problems we have today, they pale in comparison to events in the past," Meredith commented.

"I'm not sure that's true, Meredith," Ruth replied. "I think it's more accurate to say we had problems in the past and we'll have them in the future. The key is to find the right course of action. Boomers are up against a whole slew of issues, and they need a grounded approach to respond accordingly. I think they're up to the task."

It had turned into a beautiful clear night. We wandered into the club to do an inventory of the dessert table. Nothing like pecan pie and Earl Grey tea to finish off a great meal.

"There was one thing I thought a lot about this summer, an idea I got from Jamie," Pieter said as we returned to the table. "Patience is a big problem for my generation. We want things to happen now. I believe I had a problem with our investment approach because I share that impatience."

Ruth nodded in agreement. "As they age, boomers might become completely consumed by stress and impatience, but they might just learn from their experiences. There will likely be some in each camp. I'm reasonably optimistic, however: we tend to calm down as we get older. Wisdom is not wasted on the middle-aged. Their continued participation in the workforce will help stabilize them. There is a greater tendency to worry when we no longer have access to an external cash flow."

"I think they'll mellow as they age—it's inevitable," I said. "The boomers put their stamp on youth and work; they'll do the same for middle age and retirement."

"Boomers have lived through so many changes in society, such as women in the workforce and the resulting impact on married and family life," Ruth said. "Not to mention the advent of the technological age, which has had an enormous impact on so many things: the economy, our jobs, our social lives, our means of communication. Everything has happened unbelievably quickly, and the boomers have no role models to guide them on how to deal with such rapid change."

"Everything seems to lead back to the same place," I said. "In a time of rapid change and unprecedented social pressures, we all need a plan to fall back on. You need to handle the markets—have a plan. You want your life to unfold a certain way—have a plan."

"We've all learned a lot this summer, it seems, and that's great, given our current project," Ruth said.

"There's one thought I wanted to leave you with," I said. "It comes from a friend who recently passed away. He was born in India and had a wonderful way of seeing the world. He always told me that North Americans work too hard to try to be happy. Instead, they should try to be content. Happiness is fleeting, but contentedness can last a lifetime. I was struck by this observation, and I've tried to incorporate it into my life. Then, last week, I came upon a passage at the end of Michael Adams' book *Better Happy Than Rich?* A rather prophetic title. I wrote down the passage so I could give it to you: 'While the American dream seems to have something to do with achieving a feeling of importance and good fortune, I believe that Canadians aspire to a quite humbler brand of subjective well-being: simple contentment. Life in Canada is increasingly about harmony, balance, self-esteem and tolerance for diversity.'" So I feel good about Canada's future: as a nation, we're on our way.

There wasn't a whole lot more to say. I signed for dinner, and we made our escape to the parking lot. The drive home was relatively quiet. We chatted about how Dylan was doing with his job and how the new school year was going for Emily and Malcolm. But mostly we thought about what we had discussed. When we pulled up in front of the DeMarco home, Ruth and I got out of the car to give Pieter and Meredith a hug.

"You know, I'm proud of you two. You had some adversity and you faced it head-on," I said.

"With a little nudge from you, as usual," Pieter replied.

"Well, it's a two-way street: your experiences have given us great insight into what we need to tell boomers in our book," I responded.

As Pieter and Meredith turned to walk into their house, I knew we were all a little better prepared to take on whatever came our way in the future.

Further Reading

Adams, Michael. *Better Happy Than Rich? Canadians, Money and the Meaning of Life.* Toronto: Penguin Canada, 2002.

———. *Sex in the Snow: Canadian Social Values at the End of the Millennium.* Toronto: Viking Canada, 1997.

Bibby, Reginald. *Restless Gods: The Renaissance of Religion in Canada.* Toronto: Stoddart, 2002.

Bricker, Darrell and Edward Greenspon. *Searching for Certainty: Inside the New Canadian Mindset.* Toronto: Doubleday Canada, 2001.

Collins, Jim. *Good to Great: Why Some Companies Make the Leap ... and Others Don't.* New York: HarperBusiness, 2001.

Covey, Stephen R. *The Seven Habits of Highly Effective People.* New York: Free Press, 1989.

de Botton, Alain. *Status Anxiety.* Toronto: Viking Canada, 2004.

Dychtwald, Ken. *Age Power: How the 21st Century Will Be Ruled by the New Old*. New York: Jeremy P. Tarcher, 2000.

Easterbrook, Gregg. *The Progress Paradox: How Life Gets Better While People Feel Worse*. New York: Random House, 2003.

Ellis, Charles. *Winning the Loser's Game: Timeless Strategies for Successful Investing*. Third edition. New York: McGraw-Hill, 1998.

Foot, David K. and Daniel Stoffman. *Boom, Bust and Echo: How to Profit from the Coming Demographic Shift*. Toronto: Macfarlane Walter & Ross, 1996.

Galbraith, John Kenneth. *The Affluent Society*. Boston: Houghton Mifflin, 1958.

Honoré, Carl. *In Praise of Slow: How a Worldwide Movement Is Challenging the Cult of Speed*. Toronto: Knopf Canada, 2004.

MacKay, Charles. *Extraordinary Popular Delusions and the Madness of Crowds*. New York: Three Rivers Press, 1995.

Murray, Nick. *Simple Wealth, Inevitable Wealth: How Your Financial Advisor Can Grow Your Fortune in Stock Mutual Funds*. Mattituck, NY: Nick Murray, 1999.

Popcorn, Faith. *The Popcorn Report: Faith Popcorn on the Future of Your Company, Your World, Your Life*. Toronto: HarperCollins Canada, 1992.

Putnam, Robert D. *Bowling Alone: The Collapse and Revival of American Community.* New York: Touchstone, 2000.

Quindlen, Anna. *Loud and Clear.* New York: Random House, 2004.

Roadburg, Dr. Alan. *Re-tire with a Dash: The Secret to Retirement Happiness.* Niagara Falls, NY: Utd Library Publications, 2003.

————. *What Are You Doing after Work?* Niagara Falls, NY: Utd Library Publications, 2002.

Robbins, Anthony. *Awaken the Giant Within: How to Take Immediate Control of Your Mental, Emotional, Physical, and Financial Destiny.* New York: Simon & Schuster, 1991.

Rotella, Bob. *Golf Is Not a Game of Perfect.* New York: Simon & Schuster, 1995.

Schwartz, Barry. *The Paradox of Choice: Why More Is Less.* New York: Ecco, 2004.

Siegel, Jeremy. *Stocks for the Long Run: The Definitive Guide to Financial Market Returns and Long-Term Investment Strategies.* Second edition. New York: McGraw-Hill, 1998.

Worzol, Richard. *Facing the Future: The Seven Forces Revolutionizing Our Lives.* Toronto: Stoddart, 1994.

Acknowledgements

Writing, for me, is just the natural end point for ideas and issues that have been rolling around in my head. I work in an amazing business where the opportunity to discuss these ideas with clients and colleagues helps to incubate these notions. Now, as anyone who knows me would confirm, I like to discuss these ideas, and discuss and discuss. I can't help it—as a last-born, you never know when you're going to get a chance to speak again. For my clients and colleagues, I appreciate your patience and support.

Particularly I would like to thank Tim Wardrop, the manager of the Ottawa office of ScotiaMcLeod. His support and encouragement know no limits. And my colleague Peter Finnegan: It is rare to start on the same day as someone and still work together twenty years later. I hope the good-natured banter continues for another twenty years. Every good office needs a heart and a soul. I would like to thank Frank Charette for his good nature and sense of humour, and Paul White for his common sense and his wisdom.

I work with a very special group of individuals in our managed asset group. I would like to thank Willo Watson, Karen Fisher, Scott Hudson, Erin Griffiths, Catherine Clift, Alice Fang, Corrado Tiralongo and Chad Allison and last, but never, ever least, Kevin Low.

In life we always need role models, and mine is Fred Bartlett, the CEO of the Children's Hospital of Eastern Ontario Foundation. His respect for people, his sensitivity to families in need and his leadership have empowered this wonderful institution. I would simply state: I will try and always be like you.

I am surrounded by amazing people on my team. Janette Andrews has worked with me for sixteen years. Her humour and great spirit have always persevered, even in the toughest markets. Our clients are always greeted with a cheerful voice and a genuine interest in their well-being. And, of course, the outstanding Jason Brazeau. He started as a recruit fresh out of university and quickly became my Padawan. He is now, after eight years, a full partner, and I can't begin to express how grateful I am for what you do every day for our clients.

From a research perspective, I would like to thank a number of individuals who offered their insights and expertise. Frank Graves, my friend and the president of EKOS Research Associates, one of Canada's leading polling firms, revealed the social realities of the North American psyche in the post-9/11 world. Grant Schellenberg, senior analyst at Statistics Canada, gave me access to his data on the mindset of Canadians due to retire within the next ten years. My friend John Witherspoon has for years shared with me the attributes and intricacies of being an engineer. My long-time client Geoffrey Collar, another engineer, offered his insights into the history of the engineer's ring. My friend Eric Elvidge has given me great insight into the comings and goings of the high-tech world and how it impacts our investment behaviour. Thanks to David Foot

and Michael Adams, whose views of our demographic real-
ities have shaped mine for many years. And to Andrew
Smith, senior vice-president of Northern Trust Global
Advisors, for his insights into pensions and the complex
world of money management. My golf experts offered tips
on the nature of the great game: thank you to Gavin
Powers, Michael Church, David Nicol and Scott Miller.
And thanks to Bernie McDonald, one of the finest golfers
Newfoundland has produced, for his extraordinary insights
into the true nature of the game.

A number of people helped me with the ideas and
structure of this book, and to them I am grateful. Graham
Fallis and Maureen O'Brien looked through early drafts
and gave me their professional views. Michael Miske and
James McPhedran were keen supporters of this project and
offered their ideas on how to best accommodate the average
Canadian investor. David Crawford, my friend and colleague, has shared his insights for twenty years. He was
particularly helpful with the notions of tactical versus
strategic investing. As always, I owe a great deal to my
demographic literary alter ego, Susan Lightstone. A busy
schedule reduced her input from our previous books, but
her wisdom still pervades this book. To Sue Sumeraj, who
quite literally made this book come together: I am grateful
for your patience and consistency in handling my work.

I have a common boomer affliction: I never learned how
to type. While it is a challenge to write a manuscript long-
hand, it is even more of a challenge for someone to decipher
it. Many thanks to Robynne Dubeau for her patience,
precision and timely translation of my scrawl. And to all the
great people at Key Porter—Anna Porter, Meg Taylor, Lyn

Cadence, Marnie Ferguson, Paula Sloss—I have enjoyed working with you a great deal.

I would like to thank the many friends who keep me grounded and focused on what is truly important. Particularly to the members of the Presidents Dinner Club—Julie, David, Mike, Robin Victoria and Howard—who help me solve the world's problems. To my friends Jeff and Vicky, Paul and Laurie, and Mike and Lisa, who share the joys of life and family and especially cottage. To my neighbours, Jean and Judy: I have enjoyed immensely our ongoing social and political discussions, particularly the debate over who is the true poet/philosopher of our generation: Jackson Browne or Leonard Cohen. To the memory of my dear friend Kamal Dhar, who passed away this year. I will never forget the importance of being content, and simple kindness. I would like to thank Jim Minnes who, out of the blue, reminds me of the value of doing what I do. With a couple of words, the effort becomes so worthwhile.

To my mother, the respect and gratitude I have for you grow by the day, especially now that I have teenagers. And, finally, to my wonderful women, my wife, Peggy, and my daughters, Emily, Meagan and Julia: you quite literally make my life complete. Thank you for your love and support.